PRINCESS
KAIULANI

PRINCESS KAIULANI

The Last Hope of Hawaii's Monarchy

❦

KRISTIN ZAMBUCKA

Mana Publishing Company

Honolulu Hawaii

Zambucka, Kristin
    Princess Kaiulani: The Last Hope of Hawaii's Monarchy.

1. Kaiulani, Princess of Hawaii, 1875 - 1899.
2. Hawaii - Princes and princesses - Biography.
I. Title.
DU627.17.K3Z35 1982   996.9'02   82-18668

Published by Mana Publishing Company
845 Mission Lane
Honolulu, Hawaii, 96813

ISBN Soft Cover — 0-935058-02-7

"I must have been born under an unlucky star,
as I seem to have my life planned out for me
in such a way that I cannot alter it . . ."

       . . . Princess Kaiulani
       Rozel, Jersey
       In the Summer of 1897.

Princess Victoria Kaiulani 1875 - 1899

y the close of the fourteenth century, the group of islands known as Hawaii, had settled into four kingdoms individually ruled by great families of nobles known as the *alii*.

The four main islands: Oahu, Kauai, Hawaii and Maui had established rulers while ownership of smaller islands in the chain changed hands frequently as prizes of war. As closely as historians can determine, it was in the year 1758 that a chiefly child named Kamehameha was born at Kohala on the big island of Hawaii. Prophecies of greatness surrounded his birth and he emerged as the conqueror in a number of wars on all the islands. Kauai and Niihau were not conquered, but were eventually ceded to Kamehameha without a struggle.

When Captain Cook visited the islands in 1778/79, the ruling chiefs of each island were being referred to as "kings" in the European style.

King Kamehameha, victor, proceeded to restore prosperity to his island kingdom which was in a state of ruin after the long period of civil war that united all the islands. Famine and starvation had decimated the population but, by 1798, under King Kamehameha's guidance, the islands were again highly cultivated with *taro*, yams, bananas, coconuts and breadfruit growing in profusion. Industry flourished, and crime and disorder were brought under control.

The king settled on his home island of Hawaii where he made his court for many years at Kailua.

Offspring of the mighty Kamehameha I were numerous and his sons and grandsons continued to reign after him as Kings Kamehameha II, III, IV and V. But their heirs were few. The reigns of the last two Kamehamehas, grandsons of Kamehameha the Great, saw marked changes in the Hawaiian Kingdom. The two brothers both favoured a British form of government and American Missionary influence diminished in Hawaii in favour of closer ties with England.

King Kamehameha IV (Alexander Liholiho) was happily married to Emma Rooke, but their union was marred by tragedy.

The birth of their only child, Albert Edward Kauikeaouli Leiopapa, a Kamehameha, was greeted with great joy and celebration throughout the islands. Here was a newborn heir to the throne. But the little prince contracted brain fever (known today as spinal meningitis) and died in 1862 at the age of four. His untimely death shattered the King. Affected by chronic asthma and overwhelmed by grief, he too died a year later aged twenty-nine.

His brother Lot succeeded him to the throne as Kamehameha V. This last Kamehameha was thought to resemble his grandfather Kamehameha I and was described as "one of the last great chiefs of the olden type." Under his rule, many ancient *hula* and *kahuna* rituals were revived, to the horror of local Missionaries. Lot reigned for the same term as his late brother, nine years. He never married and died unexpectedly on his forty-third birthday, December 2, 1872, without naming a sucessor.

After Hawaii had been without a king for several weeks, the Cabinet decided on an election to name a new ruler. The candidates were William Charles Lunalilo and David Kalakaua both of whom had notable genealogies. Lunalilo was unanimously voted in as the new king. He was gentle and fair-minded, occasionally showing a bright intelligence and wit. But his health was weak. King Lunalilo died of tuberculosis aggravated by alcholism on February 3rd, 1874, one year and twenty-five days after coming to the throne. He benevolently willed his property to found the Lunalilo Home, a trust in perpetuity for aged and infirm Hawaiians.

An election was again vital to Hawaii's future, as there was still no heir to the vacant throne.

Queen Emma, the widow of Kamehameha IV, now contended for the rulership against David Kalakaua, who announced his candidacy the day after Lunalilo's death.

After a stormy election in which supporters of both candidates clashed heatedly, Kalakaua won by thirty-nine votes to six.

He took the oath of office on February 13th, 1874, and the colourful Kalakaua Dynasty came into being.

King Kalakaua's long reign of seventeen years brought about a resurgence of Hawaiian culture, which was characterized by the *hula* once again being danced in public, in defiance of the many oppressive laws introduced by the American Missionary element.

Kalakaua, his brother and two sisters all had a natural gift for music. They composed and sang and spent many evenings in keen, musical competition.

To his regret, Kalakaua remained childless throughout his marriage to Queen Kapiolani. His sister: Liliuokalani was also married but bore no children while his brother, William Pitt Leliohoku died of rheumatic fever at the age of twenty-two. He was unmarried. On October 16th, 1875, their sister Princess Likelike produced a precious child, Princess Victoria Kaiulani. The only niece of the king was received with great love into the family and with a burst of rejoicing throughout Hawaii.

The *alii* were dying out. The mighty line of chiefs and chiefesses that had ruled for centuries was drawing to an end. Princess Kaiulani was the last hope of the Hawaiian Monarchy, which was being undermined by foreign influences creeping with alarming swiftness into the islands. On the head of this fragile blossom rested the promise of continuity for the Hawaiian throne. The Hawaiian people looked to her for their future. This is her story. . .

After a fifty-day journey from Auckland, New Zealand, the British brig *Sisters* edged towards the old wharf at the foot of Nuuanu Avenue in the town of Honolulu.

On board were Scottish horticulturist Thomas Cleghorn, his wife and sixteen-year-old son Archie. It was June 17th, 1851.

The Cleghorns travelled to New Zealand soon after Archie's birth on November 15th, 1835, in Edinburgh, Scotland, but a stay en route in the port of Honolulu had inspired Thomas Cleghorn to return some day to the Hawaiian Islands.

Despite the barrenness of Oahu in those days, Cleghorn determined to work there as a scientific gardener introducing exotic plants to the island.

After settling his family in Honolulu, the senior Cleghorn did not obtain his desired governmental post as a scientific gardener, but instead started a dry goods store on Nuuanu Avenue between King and Hotel Streets.

Two years later, at the age of fifty-four, Thomas Cleghorn died suddenly of a heart attack while walking home from church.

His grieving widow returned to New Zealand to rejoin other family members in Auckland. But the enterprising young Archie Cleghorn stayed on in Honolulu to continue the business his father had started.

"A.S. Cleghorn and Co." was boldly painted on a newly erected sign and soon the young proprietor became a very successful merchant necessitating his move to a larger location on the corner of Queen and Kaahumanu Streets. Other branches of his firm prospered on Molokai, Maui and the big island of Hawaii.

Archie was well-liked and respected by the townspeople and became active in civic affairs. By this time he had also fathered three daughters, Helen, Rose and Annie by a handsome Hawaiian woman named Lapeka. He cherished and supported these children and kept them close to him throughout his life.

Then on September 22nd, 1870, in the reign of King Kamehameha V, Archibald Scott Cleghorn, aged 35, married Miriam Likelike, a young Hawaiian Chiefess of nineteen. The ceremony was held at Washington Place in downtown Honolulu, the family home of John Owen Dominis, who had married Likelike's sister, Liliuokalani, eight years earlier. Likelike was a descendant of one of Hawaii's ancient chiefly lines. Born on January 13th, 1851, she was the daughter of Kapaakea and Keohokalole, who were descended from the High Chief Kepookalani, first cousin to King Kamehameha I. Likelike, her sister Liliuokalani and her two brothers; Kalakaua and Leleiohuku, were known collectively by the Hawaiians as *"Na Lani Eha"*; the "Four Sacred Ones". They were extremely

Kaiulani's parents; Archibald Scott Cleghorn and Princess Miriam Likelike

Members of Kaiulani's family: Left to right (seated) Miss Laura Cleghorn (niece of A.S. Cleghorn), Princess Liliuokalani (Mrs. John O. Dominis), Princess Likelike (Mrs. A.S. Cleghorn), Mrs. Elizabeth Achuck (Keawepoole) Summer. Left to right: (standing) Mr. Thomas Cleghorn (nephew of A.S. Cleghorn), Governor John O. Dominis, Hon. Archiblad S. Cleghorn.

talented musically and composed songs that became a basic part of the Hawaiian musical repertoire. They formed their own respective glee clubs and vied with one another in a merry round of competition.

Leleiohoku died at the age of twenty-three, but Kalakaua and Liliuokalani lived to become reigning monarchs; the last two sovereigns of Hawaii.

Detailed newspaper accounts followed the honeymoon travels of the handsome couple. The Hawaiian Gazette reported:

"Soon after her marriage, Mrs. Cleghorn and her husband visited Auckland, Sydney and Melbourne. During the visit, great attention was shown to the Chiefess by the Governors and officials of the various colonies, and thus, early in life, she was brought into contact with foreign manners and ideas. Her house was, ever after, thrown open to those who visited the islands, and visitors, distinguished and otherwise, have carried her name and the memory of many kindly attentions to every country of Europe and almost every state in the Union..."

After Kalakaua became King, his brother-in-law, Cleghorn, held various government positions of increasing importance. On succeeding

Kaiulani's mother, Princess Likelike at the age of 19

Archibald Scott Cleghorn with his young wife Princess Likelike (far right) and his three daughters by a previous de facto marriage: Rose, Helen and Annie.

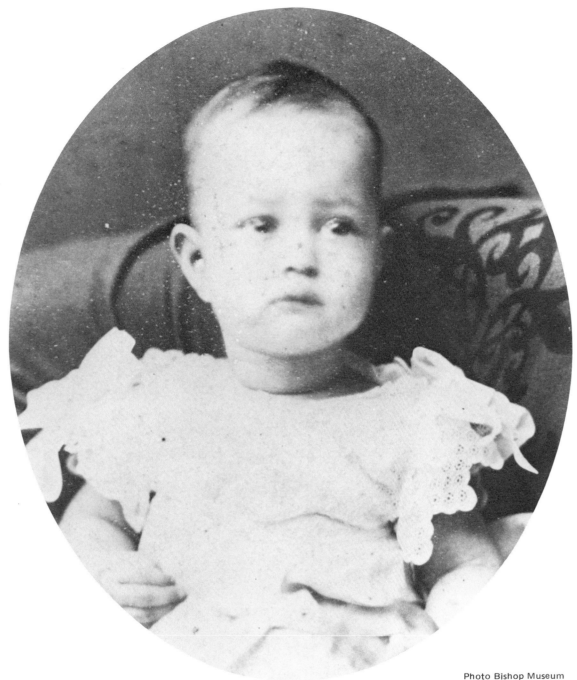

Princess Victoria Kaiulani, Kalaninuiahilapalapa Kawekiu i Lunalilo
The child born to be Queen of Hawaii.

her brother to the throne eighteen years later, Liliuokalani appointed
Archie Cleghorn as Governor of Oahu.

Five years after the Cleghorns' marriage, the only child of their
union was born on October 16th, 1875, a baby girl.

She was also the only child born to the Kalakaua dynasty and was
to become Heiress Apparent to the Hawaiian Throne which was occupied
at the time of her birth by her uncle, King Kalakaua.

The King, childless himself, was overjoyed at the arrival of his niece.
The infant's mother, Likelike was his younger sister and very dear to
him. He wanted all of Honolulu to know that she had produced an heir
to the Throne and ordered his heavy guns to fire an appropriate salute
to the Royal Child. At four o'clock in the afternoon of that October

day, all the bells of the city joined in pealing a joyous welcome that lasted for several hours. An heir had been born to the Hawaiian Throne.

One Christmas Day, 1875, in St. Andrew's Episcopal Church, Bishop Willis christened the baby: PRINCESS VICTORIA KAIULANI, KALA-NINUIAHILAPALAPA KAWEKIU I LUNALILO. She was to become known as Kaiulani which meant·"The Royal Sacred One."

Her sponsors, King Kalakaua, Queen Kapiolani and Princess Ruth, stood beside the flower-bedecked font. Kaiulani squirmed in her cashmere shawl, as her nurse Kahakukaakoi proudly held her.

Later, there was a State Reception at the old wooden place (later demolished to make way for the present Iolani Palace).

The Royal Hawaiian Band assembled on the lawn to entertain the

Photo State Archives

Captain Henry Berger around 1910

elegantly attired crowd while the bandmaster Captain Henry Berger proudly played his newly composed work entitled *"The Kaiulani March"*.

In the early years of their marriage, the Cleghorns lived in a large house on Queen Emma Street where Princess Kaiulani was born in a downstairs bedroom.

During Kaiulani's third year, they moved to reside permanently at their Waikiki property, which was four miles from the city.

Long the abode of Oahu chiefs, the property of Ainahau had many historical associations. One such notable event took place on March 20th, 1798, when Captain George Vancouver anchored his ship directly in front of the area. On coming ashore, he walked through the grounds to meet with the High Chiefs of the time.

Princess Kaiulani

riginally part of a vast estate inherited by Princess Ruth Ke-elikolani, Kaiulani's godmother, the area was called *Auaukai*. Young Mrs. Cleghorn renamed it *Ainahau* meaning "cool land", and revelled in the breezes from Manoa Valley that kept their home constantly ventilated. At Ainahau, Archie Cleghorn was able to use to the full his talent for gardening and landscaping. Years later, *Paradise of the Pacific Magazine* carried the following impressive description of the estate:

Certainly the most beautiful private estate in the Hawaiian Islands is Ainahau. The residence faces the blue Pacific and makes a graceful setting in a spacious area of highly cultivated ground. Ten acres of land are, for the most part, covered with tropical trees, shrubs and vines, the varieties of which almost bewildering, form a veritable garden that would interest a scientist. The approach to the grounds and the main entrance bear little significance of the grandeur of the premises immediately surrounding the house. A long avenue bordered by date palms and many plants leads from the gateway to the residence. Directly in front of the porch, compelling the attention of every visitor, is a majestic banyan tree, 30 years old and the parent of all the noted trees of its species in the city. With its great cluster of central trunks, enormous branches and abundant foliage, it is the King of Trees in this park, and unless destroyed by the woodman will long outlive every other form of vegetable growth in the demesne. Mr. Cleghorn cultivates eight kinds of mango trees, some of which bear the chutney mango which is so highly esteemed in India. The teak is an interesting tree that thrives here, and is now bearing seeds which are freely offered to anyone who desires to start a grove of this valuable wood. Two or three of the spice family are represented, the important one being a cinnamon. Several Washingtonia plams are here, towering almost as high as the coconuts. The latter are scattered everywhere, 500 of them having been planted when Princess Kaiulani was born.

A soap tree, indigenous to China, its fruit being used in the manufacture of saponaceous articles, is one of the novelties and an Indian tree bearing red flowers like tiger claws is another. Rubber trees thrive like lantana bushes in the open waste. Camphor is also in a healthy state of development. Monterey cypresses and date palms are numerous. Mr. Cleghorn takes pride in the 14 varieties of hibiscus he is cultivating, two varieties of the Hawaiian kamani tree and a sago palm. Importations from India are many kinds of croton.

Photo Mabel Lucas

The entrance to Ainahau (left) and to King Kalakaua's Waikiki house (right).

A view of Diamond Head from Ainahau.

A fish pond at Ainahau

The old residence at Ainahau, Waikiki

A pathway at Ainahau.

A lily pond at Ainahau

Kaiulani's pet turtle at Ainahau

In the first ballot voting for the Throne ever held in Hawaii, Kalakaua lost to King Lunalilo. Lunalilo was in poor health and reigned barely a year before his death again left the throne unoccupied.

Another election was held and this time Kalakaua won against Queen Emma, the widow of King Kamehameha IV.

Nine years and a trip-around-the-world later, Kalakaua decided that he should have a coronation ceremony as was customary with other monarchs he had met on his travels.

The date for the coronation was set for February 12, 1883.

It was a day filled with bright sunshine, and the Royal Hawaiian Band started the ceremony with the Hawaiian national anthem, "*Hawaii Ponoi.*" Although the music was composed by Bandmaster Henry Berger, the words were writted by King Kalakaua. They began:

King Kalakaua

Hawaii Ponoi
Nana I kou moi
Kalani alii
Ke alii.

Hawaii's own true sons
Be loyal to your Chief
Your country's liege and lord
The alii.

Queen Kapiolani

Iolani Palace at left and the pavillion at right. . the setting for King Kalakaua's Coronation, February 12, 1883.

Kaiulani was seven and watched the colorful scene excitedly from a window inside Iolani Palace until Mama Likelike swooped her up and rushed with her to their place in the procession that was forming in the Palace hall.

Outside, the King walked towards the pavillion in a white uniform and a white helmet topped with red, white and blue plumes that lifted in the breeze.

He wore the Order of Kamehameha on his chest plus the decorations of many foreign countries. At his side walked Queen Kapiolani in a long, red, velvet gown.

The rest of the procession followed the King and Queen with the Queen's sisters Kekaulike and Poomaikelani first and then Albert Judd, Princess Kaiulani, A.S. Cleghorn, Princess Likelike, John Dominis (Governor of Oahu) and his wife Liliuokalani.

Kaiulani's two cousins, "Koa" and "Kuhio", carried the crowns. They were later to be known as the Princes David Kawananakoa and Jonah Kuhio Kalanianaole.

Kaiulani looked closely at the crowns and saw that they were fashioned of small golden *taro* leaves encrusted with pearls, diamonds, emeralds, rubies and polished black *kukui* nuts.

In accordance with ancient Hawaiian tradition, no one was ever allowed to stand above the head of a chief nor put his hands over the head of one. Therefore, in a gesture that was badly misinterpreted by those who were ignorant of this ancient *kapu*, the King automatically picked up the crown and placed it on his own head. He then set the smaller crown on the head of Queen Kapiolani, but not without some difficulty, as her black hair had been piled up on top of her head and bejewelled for the occasion. Eight ladies-in-waiting frantically rearranged the Queen's hair-do before His Majesty could set the crown firmly in place.

Kaiulani later remarked to her governess that she thought the crown hurt the Queen as she had winced when it was jammed on her head.

Heralding the end of the ceremony, guns boomed in the distance from the decks of battleships anchored in Honolulu Harbor.

The choir filled its lungs with air and burst the tune, *"Cry Out, O Isles with Joy!"*

Hawaii had seen its first Coronation.

Guns boomed from warships anchored in Honolulu Harbour

rom the time she was seven, Kaiulani was an excellent rider, and one of the delights of her childhood was her father's gift of a white saddle pony named Fairy. With a mounted groom in attendance, she trotted around the dusty roads of Waikiki visiting friends and sometimes rode all the way into the city.

Fairy, Kaiulani's pony

Princess Kaiulani

Miss Barnes, Kaiulani's first governess, taught her to read and write and, trying out her newly acquired art, the little Princess wrote to her doting Godmother, Princess Ruth:

Dear Mama Nui,

Thank you for the nice hat you sent me. It fits so nicely. Mama wanted it, but I would not let her have it. Thank you for the corn and watermelons, they do taste so good. Are you well? With much love from your little girl.

Kaiulani

P.S. I want you to give Miss Barnes a native name.

Sounding a little annoyed with her mother, she wrote another letter:
Dear Mama Nui,

I want another hat. Mama Likelike has taken the hat you sent me. Are you better now? When are you coming home?

But "Mama Nui" didn't come home. She died on the Big Island of Hawaii in the Spring of 1883.

The young Princess Kaiulani greatly missed her godmother, who lavished affection on her and kept a constant stream of presents arriving at Ainahau.

The controversial Ruth Keelikolani, half-sister to the last Kamehameha Kings, was fiercely generous and protective towards those she loved and equally formidable towards those she disliked or mistrusted.

With her passing, many of the traditional island ways disappeared, for she was one of the last High Chiefesses of Old Hawaii.

The Island Kingdom would not see her like again.

"Mama Nui", Kaiulani's godmother, Princess Ruth Keelikolani. She was a half sister to Kings Kamehameha IV and V.

Princess Kaiulani

Princess Kaiulani

Miss Barnes, of whom the family was very fond, died unexpectedly in 1883. Many replacements were tried out, but their stays at Ainahau were short. The arrival in 1885 of Miss Gertrude Gardinier from New York was to change this pattern.

Princess Likelike approved immediately of the young woman as the new governess for her daughter who was now ten years old. Kaiulani and Miss Gardinier took to one another on sight. The young New Yorker, writing to her parents about the little Princess said: *"she is the fragile, spirituelle type, but very vivacious with beautiful large, expressive dark eyes. She proves affectionate; high spirited, at times quite willful, though usually reasonable and very impulsive and generous."*

The governess described Archibald Cleghorn as a *"man of dignified presence, a genial host devoted to his family and home and always a most courteous gentleman."*

She wrote of Princess Likelike as *"small, graceful and stylish with pretty dimpled arms and hands. She has an imperious and impulsive nature and is considered quite haughty by some, but she is very genial in her home and is always most thoughtful and considerate of those she likes."*

Kaiulani and her first governess, Miss Barnes

Photo Bishop Museum

One of Kaiulani's first letters to her father

Photo Bishop Museum

Miss Gardinier remained at Ainahau as Kaiulani's governess until the very day of her wedding to Mr. Albert Heydtmann in May, 1887.

Princess Kaiulani with Miss Gertrude Gardinier, her governess from 1885 to 1887.

Princess Kaiulani sits at the head of the table at one of her birthday parties at Ainahau.

Games at Kaiulani's birthday party at Ainahau.

Kaiulani (seated) rests during another birthday celebration at Ainahau.

Kaiulani (beneath the kahilis) at a luau with her childhood friends at Ainahau.

Kaiulani at a luau celebration at Ainahau

With childhood friends. . . at a luau at Ainahau

As 1884 began, Kaiulani's father seemed troubled by political matters. More and more he spoke with his friends of people like Lorrin Thurston, a young City lawyer whose family had been among the first Missionaries to arrive in Hawaii from New England in 1820.

Mr. Thurston has given up law to edit the Bulletin. . . he is on the side of the sugar planters who are opposing the King's party . . . what is he up to?

Always allowed to stay in the room while her father discussed politics with his friends, the young Princess sensed from their conversation, a threat to her much loved uncle, "Papa Moi".

A.S. Cleghorn

round Christmas of 1886, Mama Likelike, usually so full of life and eager to entertain their many visitors, suddenly became very quiet and withdrew completely from everyone around her.

She went to bed and refused any food that was taken to her. As Likelike grew weaker, a dark atmosphere settled over the big house at Ainahau.

Two family doctors were constantly at the Princess' bedside, but neither could diagnose anything physically wrong with her.

Her brother and sister, King Kalakaua and Princess Liliuokalani, came often to visit her and remained in the darkened room with their beloved younger sister for long periods of time.

Archibald Cleghorn sat stricken, watching the life slowly fade from his young wife. Helplessly, he turned to Liliuokalani and whispered hoarsely, *"What's wrong with her? She's only 36!"*

To further upset the family, ugly rumours were flying throughout Honolulu. *"Likelike is being prayed to death by a powerful Kahuna,"* the Hawaiian retainers at Ainahau confided to one another. But no one could believe the stories fully as everyone loved Princess Likelike. Who would want to harm her?

Then came the news that a huge school of *aweoweo*, a small, red, local fish had been seen in mid-January off the big island of Hawaii where Likelike had once been Governor. The massing of these bright red fish close to shore was always considered the harbinger of death for a member of the Kalakaua family.

A.S. Cleghorn

Princess Likelike

On the morning of February 2nd, 1887, Kaiulani was called to her mother's bedside. With a strange flash of insight, Likelike, as though to prepare Kaiulani, told her that she could see her future clearly, that she was to live away from Hawaii for a very long time, that she would never marry and that she would never be Queen.

At four o'clock that afternoon, Princess Likelike died.

Princess Likelike

The Royal party visiting John Cummins' home at Waimanalo. Kaiulani is at far left. Her aunt Liliuokalani is seated on chair next to her.

Princess Kaiulani

Princess Kaiulani

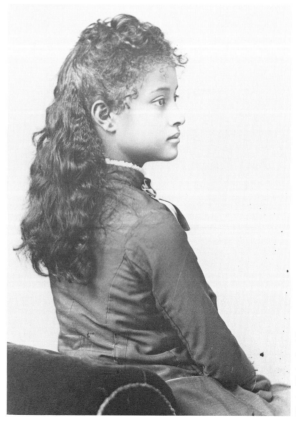

Princess Kaiulani

Princess Kaiulani

Kaiulani playing the guitar with boys from the reformatory school.

The Scottish writer, Robert Louis Stevenson.

In late January, 1889, Robert Louis Stevenson sailed into Honolulu Harbor on the yacht, *Casco*. He and his family had journeyed to Hawaii from the South Seas where the Scottish writer was known as "Tusitala, Teller of Tales." Stevenson and King Kalakaua soon struck up a boon friendship and, before too long, the King introduced him to his brother-in-law, Archie Cleghorn, a fellow Scot. Thereafter, Stevenson spent a great deal of time at Ainahau in warm camaraderie.

He was entranced with the beautiful young princess Kaiulani, and they spent many hours talking together beneath the huge banyan tree in front of the house at Ainahau.

She thought his hair was worn too long, longer than she'd seen on any Hawaiian man, and he was thinner than any of them as illness had eaten greedily into his body. But he held her attention as he told her fascinating stories about the world beyond the coral seas around her island, a world into which she was soon to venture.

Just before she left for school in England, R.L. Stevenson wrote this farewell poem in her small red autograph book:

Forth from her land to mine she goes,
The Island maid, the Island rose,
Light of heart and bright of face,
The daughter of a double race.
Her Islands here in Southern sun
Shall mourn their Kaiulani gone.
And I, in her dear banyan's shade,
Look vainly for my little maid.
But our Scots Islands far away.
Shall glitter with unwonted day,
And cast for once their tempest by
To smile in Kaiulani's eye.

The Banyan tree at Ainahau.

He added:

Written in April to Kaiulani in the April of her age and at Waikiki within easy walk of Kaiulani's banyan. When she comes to my land and her father's, and the rain beats upon the window (as I fear it will), let her look at this page; it will be like a weed gathered and preserved at home; and she will remember her own Islands, and the shadow of the mighty tree, and she will hear the peacocks screaming in the dusk and the wind blowing in the palms and she will think of her father sitting there alone.

R.L. Stevenson with King Kalakaua in Honolulu, 1889.

Aunt Liliuokalani with Robert Louis Stevenson at a luau in 1889.

King Kalakaua (straight ahead) seated beside his sister Princess Liliuokalani at a luau given for the Stevenson family in 1889.

Robert Louis Stevenson wrote that Kaiulani was: "... more beautiful than the fairest flower."

Kaiulani left for England in May, 1889. She and Stevenson never met again.

Later Stevenson wrote to his friend W. H. Low, *"I wear the colours of the little Royal maid. Oh Low, how I love the Polynesians!"*

The 13 year old Princess was fascinated by Robert Louis Stevenson.

Kaiulani "dressing up" in Japanese attire at Ainahau.

Kaiulani's half sister, Annie Cleghorn photographed on Jan. 13, 1889.

Left to right: Annie Cleghorn, Paymaster Mr. Hind, A.S. Cleghorn and Kaiulani at Ainahau.

Kaiulani "dressing up" in Japanese attire at Ainahau.

Interior of the old residence at Ainahau.

The old house at Ainahau. Kaiulani and her father are seated on the front steps at right. Other family members stand at left.

Kaiulani sitting on the railing of a bridge at Ainahau. Annie Cleghorn is at left. Family retainers in background.

Interior of the old residence at Ainahau.

Interior of the old residence at Ainahau.

In preparation for her departure, Kaiulani received the following authorization from her uncle:

I, Kalakaua, King of the Hawaiian Islands do hereby give my consent and approval for my niece Her Royal Highness Princess Victoria Kaiulani, to leave the Hawaiian Kingdom and proceed to England on or about the month of May 1889, in charge of and under the care and control of Mrs. Thomas Rain Walker and to be accompanied by Miss Annie Cleghorn.

The Princess to travel entirely incognito (crossed out) and be known as Miss Kaiulani. Her return to the Hawaiian Kingdom to be during the year of Our Lord, One Thousand and Eight Hundred and Ninety.

Signed,
KALAKAUA REX
Iolani Palace
Honolulu,
March 20th, 1889.

In April 1889, an announcement appeared in the *Honolulu Advertiser:*

Hon. A.S. Cleghorn, Collector General of Customs will accompany his daughter Princess Kaiulani on her foreign journey as far as San Francisco, leaving here May 10.

King Kalakaua

Liliuokalani seated in the front room of her residence at Washington Place.

Mrs. T.R. Walker, the wife of the British Vice-Consul, and Annie Cleghorn, the Princess' half-sister, would accompany her for the rest of the trip to England.

Her education in all subjects required for a future Queen was to begin.

For her last week in Hawaii, the Princess and her father made numerous calls around Honolulu visiting friends and relatives to say goodbye. A sleek pair of bay horses drew the Cleghorns' carriage, and a footman stood on a box at the back.

They called on cabinet members, clergymen, consulates and private homes. Kaiulani's ex-governess, Miss Gardinier, now married, had her first baby. The princess visited her, held the infant in her arms and wiped her tears away as she kissed them both goodbye.

The last call on their rounds was made to the King and Queen at Iolani Palace. "Mama" and "Papa Moi" bade a warm farewell to their niece as did Aunt Liliuokalani at Washington Place. But the most tears shed that day were for Fairy as she hugged the gentle white pony that had brought so much joy to her childhood.

At noon on Friday, May 10, the S.S. *Umatilla* sailed for California with the 13 year old Princess on board. Kaiulani, trying to hold back her tears, clung to the wooden railing in front of her. As the ship edged away from the wharf, a huge multi-coloured crowd stood waving hands and handkerchiefs and calling out blessings and farewells.

Faces loved and familiar began to blur as the ship headed out to sea. The band from a distance sounded metallic and brassy as it played the last strains of the National Anthem, *Hawaii Ponoi*. A knot of people, miniaturized with distance, clustered on the wharf as the watery gulf grew wider.

Honolulu harbour in the 1880's.

Princess Kaiulani

Kaiulani looked beyond the shore to the majestic blue-green mountains behind Honolulu that stood proudly with clouds, for capes, around their shoulders.

With stinging eyes, she tore herself away from the scene and hurried to her cabin. Annie Cleghorn and Mrs. Walker hastened to comfort her, but saw that it would be best to leave her alone with her thoughts.

After a rough, week-long crossing to San Francisco, Papa left Kaiulani there and returned to Honolulu. After his departure, Kaiulani's tears didn't dry until the train ride across the States brought her to the sprawling, bustling city of New York. Its size was beyond her imagination.

Kaiulani photographed in San Francisco in 1889 on her way to school in England.

Kaiulani photographed in San Francisco May 1889 . . . on her way to school in Europe.

From New York, Kaiulani sailed to Liverpool with her companions. (Mrs. Walker had her two small children with her also.) They disembarked and took the train to Manchester, the smoky midland city, where they spent their first night in England. It was a long way from the soft, balmy air of the Hawaiian Isles.

On June 18, they finally reached the city of London. From there, Kaiulani penned excited letters to "Mama and Papa Moi" describing her visits to the theatres of the West End; art galleries where she was awestruck by the huge canvases of Titian, Rubens and Reynolds; the Crystal Palace and the Tower of London, that bleak stone structure where ravens seemed ever watchful of its visitors. She thought of the young English Princes imprisoned within cold stone walls so long ago and Sir Walter Raleigh writing the *History of the World* in that dark cramped room that seemed to her "like a cave".

"I am going to school in the middle of September," she wrote to friends back home. *"The name of the School is Great Harrowden Hall in Northamptonshire."*

It was here at Harrowden Hall in Northamptonshire, England, that Kaiulani attended schoolroom classes for the first time. She had previously been tutored by governesses.

Harrowden Hall, built in the fifteenth century for the Barons Vaux, is located two miles outside the village of Wellingborough and 68 miles north of London.

It became a private school for young ladies in the 1890s under the guidance of Mrs. Sharp, the headmistress.

Photo Evening Telegraph - Wellingborough

Kaiulani's school in England. . . Great Harrowden Hall.

Photo Evening Telegraph - Wellingborough

Great Harrowden Hall, 2 miles outside Wellingborough, Northamptonshire, 68 miles north of London.

Kaiulani in England. . . always awaiting news from home.

n October of 1890, while at school at Harrowden Hall, Kaiulani received a mysterious letter from her uncle, King Kalakaua. Much of its meaning was a riddle to her, as he began by questioning her about her life at school, then proceeded to warn her to *"be on guard against certain enemies I do not feel free to name in writing."* Who was it? Whom did he fear?

15 year old Kaiulani wrote back to him at once, expressing her bewilderment. *"I am quite at a loss to know to whom you refer as not to be relied upon—I wish you could speak more plainly, as I cannot be on my guard unless I know to whom you allude."* She continued with a mention of the kindness of her guardian Mr. Davies, saying between the lines, *"surely you don't refer to him!"*

She anxiously awaited her Uncle's reply, but no explanation ever came.

The King who was beginning to worry those around him because of the illness now showing in his face, left for San Francisco in November, hoping the change would do him some good. He named his sister, Liliuokalani, Regent in his absence.

Two months later, Kalakaua died in San Francisco at the Palace Hotel.

Kalakaua on the *Charleston* bound for San Francisco, November 1890.

Liliuokalani on the day she was proclaimed Queen, succeeding her dead brother King Kalakaua. Photo taken at Iolani Palace, Jan 30th, 1891. She was 53. Inset is Liliuokalani's husband, John Owen Dominis.

One of the last photos taken of King Kalakaua, just before his death in San Francisco on January 20, 1891. He was 55.

Iolani Palace draped in black for King Kalakaua's funeral on February 15, 1891. In the throne room, services were conducted by the Episcopal Bishop of Honolulu, the Reverend Alfred Willis.

Many years later, after much disillusionment at the hands of "trusted people", Kaiulani realized the significance of her Uncle's warning.

Writing to her Aunt Liliuokalani, on the death of her Uncle, the news of which had just reached her by cable:

Sundown
Hesketh Park
Southport

Dear Auntie,

*I have only just heard the sad news from San Francisco. I cannot tell my feelings just at present, but Auntie, you can think how I feel. I little thought when I said goodbye to my dear Uncle nearly two years ago that it would be the last time I should see his dear face. Please give my love to Mama Moi (*Queen Kapiolani*), and tell her I can fully sympathize with her.*

I cannot write any more, but Auntie, you are the only one left of my dear Mother's family, so I can ask you to do that little thing for me.

I must close with love and kisses,

I remain,

Your loving niece,
Kaiulani

Jan. 21st., 1891.

In September she received a letter from home concerning yet another death, that of her Aunt Liliuokalani's husband, John Owen Dominis:

Washington Place.
Sept. 18th, 1891.

My Dear Kaiulani,

You have heard e'er this of the death of your dear Uncle John, from Mrs. Robertson.

I could not write at the time to tell you, for I was so shocked. It all seemed so sudden to me. It is true he had been sick ten weeks but I had no idea he would pass away so soon, for he looked so well that morning. I seems we are having a series of sadness in our family for it is only seven months since my dear Brother died, when my husband was taken away—not that only but a short time before Uncle John's death the Queen Dowager Kapiolani had a stroke of paralysis and is likely to have another.

If it is the father's will in Heaven I must submit for the Bible teaches us "he doeth all things well".

You and Papa are all that is left to me.

I shall look forward to the time when you could finish your studies with all due satisfaction to your teachers, and then come home and live a life of usefulness to your people. My health is pretty good considering all that I had to go through.

In 1892, rumours reached Kaiulani in England that the Queen would appoint Prince David Kawananakoa to succeed her late husband as Governor of Oahu.

Writing from the Davies' family residence that overlooked the Irish Sea, she pleaded with her Aunt: *I hear from many people, that David is to have the Governorship. Please do not think me very forward, but I should so like Father to have it. I have not asked you for anything before, but if you can possible grant this, I should be so grateful.*

Further on, in the same letter: *When I come home I shall try to help you as much as I can, tho it will not be much as I don't understand State Affairs. Father is going to try to get home as fast as he can, as he may be of some use to you. He was quite unwell last Tuesday. The evening before, he went into the slums of London with a detective, as he wished to see how the police did their work. He did not get home till after one o'clock, so the consequence was he was laid up the next day. The doctor said that the smells had been too much for him...*

Her deep love and concern for her father shows as she pleads further with her Aunt:

. . . I hear that you wish Father to be Governor, but to give up the Customs House. Auntie, we cannot do without his salary for that, as the salary of Governor is only half the other. My education and stay in England is costimg him something, and Oh Auntie! I do not want him to get into debt. Please do not be offended with me...

Kaiulani (seated front left) is visited in England by Papa (seated in centre).

Mrs. Rooke's house, No. 7 Cambridge Road, Brighton, where Kaiulani was privately tutored in German, English, French and music. After leaving her school Great Harrowden Hall.

Cambridge Road, Brighton, today. No. 7 is the first house past the church.

On leaving Great Harrowden Hall. . .

Sundown,
Hesketh Park,
Southport.

Dear Auntie,

Thank you so much for your kind letter. It is very good of you to write to me, as I know how very busy you must be with State Affairs.

I am so glad to see that Father is putting up a proper house at Ainahau. It has always been my ambition to have a house at Waikiki worthy of the beautiful garden.

I hope that you liked my photographs.

I have left Great Harrowden Hall for good, Mr Davies has kindly found a lady who will look after, and be sort of mother to me while I am in Brighton. I believe Mrs. Rooke is a thorough lady.

I shall take lessons in French, German, music and English, especially grammar and composition. I am anxiously waiting for the time to come when I may see you again.

I must close this short letter,
With much love, Believe me,
Your affectionate niece,
Victoria Kaiulani.
Feb. 5th, 1892.

Kaiulani was unaware of the trouble that was building up at home between the Royalists and the "Annexation Club" which had been secretly formed in 1892.

Dan Logan was now the editor of the *Bulletin* and he spoke out fearlessly against the "traitorous sugar barons" who would see the Monarchy overthrown for their own monetary gain. (Logan was eventually silenced when he was arrested on a charge of libel filed by American Minister John L. Stevens who was a dedicated Annexationist.)

Great tension mounted in Honolulu as the Queen spoke out against her enemies. Concerned for her safety, a group of loyal young Hawaiians led by the six Irish-Hawaiian Lane brothers, appointed themselves round-the-clock guardians of Queen Liliuokalani and took up posts at Iolani Palace.

Photo Bishop Museum

Princess Kaiulani.

Kaiulani (seated right front) with friends at school in England.

On March 20th, Kaiulani wrote to her Aunt from 7 Cambridge Road in Brighton, Sussex, where she was now in the care of Mrs. Rooke:

> *Brighton is such a nice place, though I have only been here a month, I can find my way about quite easily. I think that I shall profit by my stay here in many ways. The air is very pure and bracing and already my appetite shows me that it suits me.*
>
> *I am taking lessons in music, singing, literature, history, French and German. I have such a nice lady for a singing mistress. She has taught me such a lot, and she says that I have a very sweet soprano voice—I think that I must have inherited it from you. I am getting on pretty well with my music, and I am so fond of it.*
>
> *I have enjoyed my studies very much during the last term, and I feel that I am learning something. I can speak German quite fluently, though I make a great many mistakes. I do not feel so very nervous about it as I used to do.*
>
> *I hope that Father will allow me to stay here till Christmas, then let me travel about on the continent for a month or two before I "Come out" in society.*
>
> *I am looking forward to my return next year. I am beginning to feel very homesick—I shall be very glad to see you. I suppose that you will not know me again as I have changed so much."*

April 19th, 1892:

We are starting for Jersey tomorrow, the boat leaves at 12 o'clock at night so we shall have to start pretty early in the afternoon so that we can get comfortably settled.

We go via Southampton. It only takes nine hours to get there, but I believe that it is very rough between Guernsey and Jersey. Mrs. Rooke's house is not very large but her garden is very beautiful. I intend to enjoy my holiday as much as I possibly can, so that I may come back to my studies quite refreshed. We are having very cold weather at the present moment. Last week it was so warm that we all went out of doors without any jackets at all. I must say that I prefer the intense cold to the intense heat.

After a very rough voyage across to Jersey that took two hours longer than usual, Kaiulani was very ill, but managed to write to her Aunt:

The drive to St. Helier to Mrs. Rooke's little house at Rozel quite refreshed me.

On the 26th, still holidaying in Jersey, she wrote:

The weather is quite perfect and altogether this place reminds me very much of home. I wish I was there now. V.K.

Kaiulani, the schoolgirl wearing spectacles, photographed by London Stereoscopic Co., Regent Street West.

Kaiulani dressed up for the cold of England's midlands.

Also written from Brighton:

Last Saturday I had my first lesson in dancing and general deportment which I found highly amusing. My friends tell me that I carry myself so much better when I am walking in the street then in a drawing room, so at the present moment I am doing my very best to walk into a room quietly and gracefully.

To her Aunt:

Brighton
May 18, 1892

It is so warm here, I wear white thin blouses all day. They are so very comfortable and cool. The only thing I miss is my riding horse. I would give almost anything if I could have Fairy to ride. Very few people ride here and their horses are so very poor, I would not ride them if they were offered to me.

I am having such very pretty Summer dresses made. I like pretty, dainty things. All the ladies are wearing dresses made like men's clothes. I do dislike them as they look so very manly.

Princess Kaiulani

Photo State Archives

7 Cambridge Road
Brighton
Oct. 25, 1892

My Dear Aunt,

I hope that you will not think me impertinent in asking you for one of your photographs. I have not got one of you.

My room is very pretty but I think a few photos would improve it. At present I have only two—one of Mother and one of Father.

On my birthday Mrs. Rooke gave me "The Soul's Awakening", it is such a beautiful picture. I have always wished to have it, but I have never had enough money. It hangs opposite my bed so that the first thing I see in the morning is the girl's lovely face. I received quite a number of presents and such a lot of letters. I spent a very happy day in spite of being such a long way from home.

n January 14th, 1893, Queen Liliuokalani informed her Cabinet Ministers that she intended to form a new Constitution which would restore full power to the Monarchy and rights to the Hawaiian people. The Ministers wasted no time in betraying her and scurried downtown with the information to the "Committee of Safety". The "Committee" comprised a group of foreign businessmen, mostly American, and was formed solely for the purpose of overthrowing the Monarchy and annexing Hawaii to the United States.

They promptly made arrangements with the American Minister, John L. Stevens, to land marines from the *U.S.S. Boston* in Honolulu upon call. The *Boston* was anchored just offshore and with its huge cannon and well-trained troops, was an ominous threat to this small sovereign nation that depended on a handful of household guards for protection.

Two days later, on the afternoon of the 16th, that threat became a reality when marines scrambled ashore and marched through the streets of Honolulu.

Hawaiians suddenly realized that the possibility of a coup was at hand and an alarmed Queen's Cabinet held a hurried meeting with Governor Cleghorn of Oahu to discuss this shocking event.

Honolulu in the early 1890's. The view from Iolani Palace towards Punchbowl. . . Washington Place concealed in trees.

Photo State Archives

Queen Liliuokalani

Photo State Archives

Governer of Oahu. Archibald Scott Cleghorn.

Photo State Archives

U.S. Minister John L. Stevens.

The "Annexation Club" called a meeting at the Armory, which drew more than a thousand people. "Annexationist" speakers declared that the Hawaiian Islands were in danger of a "bloody revolution".

Lorrin Thurston stood up and said it was Queen Liliuokalani's fault and emphasized this point by shouting: *"Now is the time to act and overthrow this disgusting Monarchy!"*

Judge Sanford Ballard Dole, a cooler voice in this heated assembly, suggested that, rather than abrogate the Monarchy entirely, the Queen should be asked to retire in favour of her niece, Princess Kaiulani, and act as an advisor to the Throne along with a regency composed of other prominent Hawaiians. He added that Hawaii would then be fully supported by England and the United States and that the Hawaiians would *"not lose their Government under such a plan."*

The "Committee" rejected Dole's plan and insisted that a new government be formed with Dole himself at its head. He finally agreed and U.S. Minister Stevens notified the Queen that a Provisional Government had been formed.

On the 17th, at 5:00 p.m., a delegation from the newly formed Provisional Government called on the Queen at Iolani Palace and demanded her immediate abdication.

The Queen's Cabinet. . .

Samuel Parker Minister of Foreign Affairs (lower left)
John F. Colburn Minister of the interior (top left)
William H. Cornwell Minister of Finance (top right)
Arthur P. Peterson Attorney General (lower right)

With armed Marines patrolling the streets and the threat of American military intervention that they represented, she realized the futility of resistance and prepared the following document for the PGs:

I, Liliuokalani, by the grace of God and under the Constitution of the Hawaiian Kingdom, Queen, do hereby solemnly protest against any and all acts done against myself and the Constitutional Govt., of the Hawaiian Kingdom by certain persons claiming to have established a provisional Government of and for this Kingdom. That I yield to the superior force of the United States of America whose Minister Plenipotentiary, His Excellency John L. Stevens, has caused the United States troops to be landed at Honolulu and declaring he would support such a provisional government.

Now to avoid collision of armed forces and perhaps loss of life, I do, under this protest and impelled by such forces, yield my authority until such time as the Government of the United States shall upon the facts being presented to it, undo the action of its representative and reinstate me in the authority which I claim as the Constitutional Sovereign of the Hawaiian Islands.

Done at Honolulu this 17th day of January, 1893.

Judge Hartwell was the last witness to leave the room. He shook the Queen's hand with tears welling in his eyes. Mrs. Wilson, the Queen's lady-in-waiting, scoffed as he left: "Crocodile tears."

That night, Honolulu was rocked by the worst earthquake ever recorded in the islands. . . Talk flew amongst the Hawaiians that the Goddess Pele was outraged at what had happened.

The Queen wrote later:

After those in my place of imprisonment had all affixed their signatures, they left, with the single exception of Mr. A.S. Hartwell. As he prepared to go, he came forward, shook me by the hand, and the tears streamed down his cheeks. This was a matter of great surprise to me. After this he left the room. If he had been engaged in a righteous and honorable action, why should he be affected? Was it the consciousness of a mean act which overcame him so? Mrs. Wilson, who stood behind my chair throughout the ceremony, made the remark that those were crocodile's tears. I leave it to the reader to say what were his actual feelings in the case. . .

Photo State Archives

Samuel M. Damon of the Committee of Safety's Advisory Council.

Lawyer Alfred S. Hartwell who drew up the document for Liliuokalani to sign.

Badly shaken by the takeover, Cleghorn wrote his opinion of the Queen's actions to Kaiulani:

It is the first time in 16 days I have called. I had called once before but her people said she was resting—as a rule I try to visit her once a week.

Since the 17th January I have no pleasure in talking with her, as she is to blame for all our troubles.

Has she written you since the 17th Jan.? If not please say so in your answer to this.

He wrote further:

If the Queen had abdicated the night of the 16th or early on the 17th, the Throne I think could have been saved. But she did not think they would do as they did, she still followed the advice of poor Ministers' wretched wills, and we have all to suffer.

I visited her several times that day, 17th, and told her there would be a Provisional Government. Still she held on—and one hour after, the Committee called and told her they had the Government in their hands. To have resisted would only have cost a lot of lives, and made things worse.

Photo Bishop Museum

Princess Kaiulani

Prince David Kawananakoa

On January 18, the PGs decided to send five commissioners to Washington to arrange a "quick annexation" of the Hawaiian Islands.

To counteract this move, Liliuokalani sent attorney Paul Neumann and Prince David Kawananakoa to defend the Monarchy on her behalf.

In England on Jan. 30th, 1893, Kaiulani's guardian Mr. Theophilus H. Davies received three telegrams. One said, "Queen Deposed"; the second read "Monarchy Abrogated"; and the third asked Mr. Davies to: "Break News to Princess."

Kaiulani was stunned. Mr. Davies suggested that Kaiulani make an immediate trip to Washington to plead Hawaii's case with the newly elected President, Grover Cleveland. He and his wife would accompany her.

Lawyer Paul Neumann

Kaiulani, in her 18th year, was still shy of the political world. At first she said she couldn't face such an ordeal but, on thinking it over, she decided: *"Perhaps someday the Hawaiians will say that Kaiulani could have saved us but she didn't even try! I will go with you."*

In February, Princess Kaiulani issued a statement through the London newspapers which read:

> *Four years ago, at the request of Mr. Thurston, then a Hawaiian Cabinet Minister, I was sent away to England to be educated privately and fitted to the position which by the Constitution of Hawaii I was to inherit. For all these years I have patiently and in exile striven to fit myself for my return this year to my native country. I am now told that Mr. Thurston is in Washington asking you to take away my flag and my throne. No one tells me even this officially. Have I done anything wrong, that this wrong should be done to me and my people? I am coming to Washington to plead for my throne, my nation and my flag. Will not the great American people hear me?*

Princess Kaiulani with her gaurdian Mr. Theo. H. Davies in Boston, March 1893.

Kaiulani in Boston, March 1893

A few days later, the Princess sailed for the United States on the *Teutonic*, accompanied by Mr. and Mrs. Davies, their daughter Alice, a chaperone and a maid.

Arriving March 1st in New York harbour, Kaiulani had prepared a statement which she read to the newspaper reporters and hordes of people who swarmed over the pier for a glimpse of the Princess who might become an American citizen if her homeland were annexed.

Unbidden I stand upon your shores today where I had thought so soon to receive a royal welcome. I come unattended except for the loving hearts that come with me over the winter seas. I hear the Commissioners from my land have been for many days asking this great nation to take away my little vineyard. They speak no word to me, and leave me to find out as I can from the rumours of the air that they would leave me without a home or a name or a nation.

Seventy years ago, Christian America sent over Christian men and women to give religion and civilization to Hawaii. Today three of the sons of those missionaries are at your capitol, asking you to undo their fathers' work. Who sent them? Who gave them the authority to break the Constitution which they swore they would uphold?

Today, I, a poor weak girl, with not one of my people near me and all these statesmen against me, have strength to stand up for the rights of my people. Even now I can hear their wail in my heart, and it gives me strength and courage and I am strong...strong in the faith of God, strong in the knowledge that I am right, strong in the strength of seventy million people who in this free land will hear my cry and will refuse to let their flag cover dishonour to mine!

Critics in Honolulu laughed at the Princess' appeal saying that Mr. Davies wrote every statement she made, while mainland newspaper accounts published the next day glowed with descriptions of Kaiulani. One said:

"The Princess is a tall beautiful young woman of sweet face and slender figure."

Another wrote: *"The Princess impresses one as tall and slight with decidedly good eyes which are soft brown. Her hair is almost black and somewhat wavy. Her complexion is dark but not more so than many girls whom one meets every day on Broadway."*

During her brief visits to Boston and Washington, writers continued to enthuse, writing that *"whenever Kaiulani passed through hotel dining rooms, comments of admiration are heard on all sides."*

Kaiulani in Boston, 1893

The five Annexation Commissioners in 1893

Top, left to right: L.A. Thurston, W.R. Castle, C.L. Carter. Lower, left to right: W.C. Wilder, J. Marsden.

Finally, on March 13, 1893, Princess Kaiulani was received at the White House by President Grover Cleveland and his wife, who was popularly known as "the White House Bride". Twenty five years younger than her husband, the President's wife was greatly loved by the American people.

Kaiulani later commented on how "sweet and beautiful" Mrs. Cleveland was and added that the President was "entertaining".

The mention of politics was carefully avoided, but President Cleveland managed to convey to the princess that he meant to see justice done to her and her country. Kaiulani also hoped to counteract some of the vicious propaganda written by the PGs in which they accused Hawaii's rulers of being "undisciplined savages."

Commissioners from Hawaii's Provisional Government were in Washington pushing as hard as they could for the Annexation Bill to pass.

Captain G. E. Wiltse U.S.N. Commander of the U.S. Cruiser *Boston* that landed troops in Honolulu on January 17, 1893.

Captain Wiltse, bedecked with flower leis, leaving for San Francisco a few months later.

Lawyer Lorrin A Thurston at age 29, the grandson of "First Company" Protestant Missionary, Asa Thurston.

Theophilus Davies mentioned to reporters: *"Over Wormley's Hotel where the Provisional Government Commissioners are stopping, I noticed this morning, gentlemen, that the Hawaiian flag is flown. Yet I am told that the American flag flies over the Honolulu Government Buildings. A curious state of affairs!"*

When Kaiulani arrived in Washington, Prince David Kawananakoa was already there working with Paul Neumann (the deposed Queen's lawyer). In a gallant effort to combat the distorted picture of the Hawaiian Monarchy that was deliberately painted by the PGs and to regain the Throne for Liliuokalani, Kawananakoa told reporters that *"it seemed that Kaiulani was influenced by Mr. Davies in coming to America."* The Prince stated further: *"Mr. Davies is working against the interests of the Queen, which is in bad taste to say the least."*

Iolani Palace on King Street, Honolulu in the early 1890's.

Despite his disapproving attitude, Prince David made a courtesy call on Kaiulani at Brevoort House in New York where she and her party had rented suites.

But, as Kaiulani and Mr. and Mrs. Davies had heard of his remarks regarding their visit, he was only allowed to talk to the Princess for a few minutes, and that at 10:00 o'clock at night when he was finally admitted to her suite at the tail-end of a stream of callers.

Regardless of the rift that existed between Kaiulani and Kawananakoa, the newspapers still feasted on their imagined engagement, one reporting that the Princess' "fiance", Prince David, was waiting to greet her on her arrival in New York.

Copy from *The Mail* and *Express Bureau* in Washington, D.C., on March 8, 1893, read:

The Princess Kaiulani arrived this morning from Boston. The train was late and although she was due at the Arlington at 10:30 o'clock, she did not arrive until after 12. There were very few to receive her, but Prince David was on hand to welcome his fiancee.

The Princess looked tired after her journey. She was dressed in a dark travelling costume and a big broad blue hat. Around her neck was a garland of La France roses and smilax reaching to her waist. As she entered the Hotel with Mr. and Mrs. Davies, Prince David rushed to the front door and shook her by the hand. The Princess was at once shown to her apartments on the second floor.

What will be done officially in presenting her case to the State Dept. has not been decided. The Hawaiian Annexation treaty is not dead. Unless President Cleveland shall withdraw it from the Senate as he did the Nicaragua Canal treaty soon after he entered the Presidency in 1885, it will continue 'alive' for action by the Senate at the pleasure of that body. There are many Senators here who say the Princess has hurt her own cause by coming here. Mr. Cleveland has been silent so far in regard to his feeling toward the question, but it is thought before many days he will bring the matter before the Senate again.

Princess Kaiulani in 1893

On the same morning of Kaiulani's visit to President Cleveland, he announced that he would send a special investigator to report on the situation in Hawaii. By his receiving Princess Kaiulani, he underscored his sympathy towards the plight of the Hawaiian Monarchy. The PG commissioners were furious, as the President's appointment of an investigator would now hinder their well laid plans to rush Annexation through "as quickly as possible, with no questions asked."

Washington papers were full of speculation both for and against Annexation; after all, American property interests in Hawaii were now very great. Rumors buzzed about as they tried to guess whom the President would appoint as his personal investigator.

President Grover Cleveland in 1893

On March 15, Mr. Davies, ever loyal to Hawaii, addressed the public regarding the situation:

One of the saddest features of this matter is that it has been presented as a plot and a conspiracy of bad men. It is not that. It is the blunder of good men, men to many of whom I would entrust my dearest interests. They have been goaded on by misrule into injustice, forgetting that injustice is not remedy for misrule. Today the Provisional Government of Hawaii dares not appeal to the Electorate to ratify any one of their acts. What kind of Government is that?

Within a couple of days, President Cleveland announced that ex-Congressman James H. Blount of Georgia was to sail immediately on the cutter *Rush* for Honolulu, and make a full report on the situation there. The President also conferred on Blount paramount authority over any other American official in the Hawaiian Islands. He quickly became known as "Paramount Blount".

Photographed in April 1893. . . the USRC Cutter *Rush* that brought Commissioner James Blount to Hawaii.

The arrival in Honolulu of U.S. Commissioner Blount in April 1893.

Commissioner and Mrs. Blount in Honolulu 1893.

It seemed to Kaiulani that America had finally come to care about the fate of her Islands and before she and the Davies family returned to England where she was to continue her studies for an indefinite period, she issued a farewell statement to the American Press:

Before I leave this land, I want to thank all whose kindnesses have made my visit such a happy one. Not only the hundreds of hands I have clasped nor the kind smiles I have seen, but the written words of sympathy that have been sent to me from so many homes, has made me feel that whatever happens to me I shall never be a stranger to you again. It was to all the American people I spoke and they heard me as I knew they would. And now God bless you for it—from the beautiful home where your fair First Lady reigns to the little crippled boy who sent his loving letter and prayer.

During her entire visit newsmen enthused in their descriptions of Kaiulani: "delicate beauty, with exquisitely small, well shaped hands, an accomplished musician, an artist, a linguist with the genteel manners of a born aristocrat." The derogatory comments spread by the PGs regarding the Monarchy began to appear somewhat ridiculous and most leading American newspapers now became very outspoken in their support of the Royalist cause.

A few newspapers remained distinctly pro-Annexation, energized by the picture the PGs had painted. But the influential *New York Times* called for a "complete investigation" in the Hawaiian Islands, while the *St. Louis Chronicle* said the revolution in Hawaii was not "by the people but by those who were not permitted by Queen Liliuokalani to plunder the land."

Harper's Magazine spoke strongly against Annexation and the "tricks" of the PGs while the *New York Herald* flatly stated: "Mr Thurston's threat to deliver the Islands to England if the treaty is not ratified, is not quite nice."

Constant harrassment by the press in Hawaii continued as the *Pacific Commercial Advertiser* in April of 1893 published a story telling readers that, "ex-Princess Kaiulani is really engaged to be married to a son of Theo. H. Davies. The young gentleman in question, Mr. Clive Davies, is now studying in Boston. It is stated that he admits his betrothal with the ex-Princess. It is well known that Kaiulani was often a guest of Mr. Davies in his home in Southport, England, and the prospect of the union would account in some measure for the extraordinary zeal lately displayed by Mr. Davies on behalf of the ex-Princess."

The rumours of the "engagement" had probably been fanned by Kaiulani's visit, the month before, to Boston's Institute of Technology where young Clive was studying. (She was accompanied by Clive Davies' parents.) The Princess instantly charmed the young men in Clive's class at the College, many of whom were so smitten that they followed her to other appointments around the city.

Meanwhile, Papa, at home at Ainahau, repeatedly and sometimes gruffly, denied the rumoured romance. "There is not a word of truth in it!" Cleghorn said. "It is absurd!"

Cleghorn wrote from Honolulu on April 8th, 1893:
I have placed two snapshots in a frame and they are still at Williams photo place in Fort St., so that the people can see them. I called on your Aunt this afternoon and showed her some of them —she did not say anything—I do not and cannot understand her— I think for the present you are better not here, much as I would like to have you home, still things must be settled soon, and then we will know what to do. Has your Aunt written you since the 16th of January?

Princess Kaiulani

Papa kept her faithfully informed of developments at home and in another letter, written in May, he says:

> *Blount is a busy man taking in all, in regard to our troubles. I have not had a talk with him yet. I think I wrote you that I called on him the day after his arrival, but the Captain of the Ship was present, so I did not talk politics—What his upset will be here, who knows for he never gives anyone any idea of his plans.*
>
> *Spreckels and his family are here and he is opposed to Annexation, but a friend of his told me he wanted a Republic, and that would be better than Annexation to the States, at least I think so.*

Again from Cleghorn in 1893:

> *Mr. Blount the Commissioner from President Cleveland is hard at work processing all the information he can. I have not had a talk with him yet. He paid your Aunt his first visit yesterday. He was coming out of Washington Place as I was going in.*

May 11, 1893:

> *L.A. Thurston has been appointed by the PG as Minister to Washington. He will work all he knows for Annexation. The papers here are very annoying. They do write such nasty articles. We have one in particular the Star. That paper was started for the Annexation Club and they do write such nasty things. I spend long days at Ainahau. . .*

On the 24th of May, the Queen wrote to Kaiulani informing her that she was to be offered the Throne:

Queen Liliuokalani seated in the grounds of Washington Place on Beretania Street. Colonel Sam Nowlein in background.

My Dear Kaiulani,

I simply write to assure you that we are well and Papa seemed in good health but I think looks a little thin.

I hear from some parties that your house is looking fine, but Mr. Robertson says he has not ever seen it."

Kaiulani's Aunt continues with the real purpose of the letter:

I would simply like to add and say that should anyone write or propose or make any proposition to you in any way in regard to taking the Throne, I hope you will be guarded in your answer. The people all over the Islands have petitioned to have me restored and it would make you appear in an awkward light to accept any overtures from any irresponsible party, and the PGs are growing less and less, and I understand they will soon drop to pieces as the saying is, for want of funds to carry on the Govt. Mr. Spreckels will not help them or loan them any money and Bishop and Co. would not loan them any money without Mr. Spreckels—and now we are waiting patiently till the US Commissioner in Mr. Stevens' place, could tell us we are free. I will write you and acquaint you of all that transpires, and if need be will advise you after consulting with your father.

Later, on June 1st, Liliuokalani writes apologizing for the above "hurried note" as she was getting ready to receive a young Indian Prince, the Nawab of Kampur. She said that as the Prince was leaving he remarked to some Hawaiians: "Why did her people permit her to be deposed?"

The Queen explains:

Come to think of it, my dear Kaiulani, it was treachery on the part of my Ministers. (and it helped the agitation backed by the US troops)—that was why, but don't mention this. It would not be well if it came from your lips—we have to act with policy.

She replied to her Aunt from the Yews, Kettering, on June 15:

I have never received any proposals from anybody to take the Throne. I have not received a word of any sort from anyone except my father. I am glad that I am able to say that I have not written to anyone about politics.

I have been perfectly miserable during the past four months. I have looked forward to '93 as being the end of my "exile". I have considered the four years I have been in England as years of exile. Now is seems as though things would never settle and I am simply longing to see you all—People little know how hard it is to wait patiently for news from home. Mr. Davies is very kind and sends me all the information he can, but I suppose we shall not get any real news as to the settlement of affairs for months. In the meantime, "il faut attendre."

I am staying with my old school mistress Mrs. Sharp. She gave up her school (Great Harrowden Hall) two years ago, and is now living in a dear little home of her own.

I am as happy as I can possibly be under the circumstances.

I am really and truly recruiting my health which has not been good lately.

I do a good deal of hard reading, practising, sewing and gardening."

In Honolulu, on June 2, 1893, the PGs took over Iolani Palace as their headquarters and renamed it the "Executive Building."

"The Yews" at Burton Latimer, Kettering, the cottage Princess Kaiulani rented, 8 miles from her old school, Great Harrowden Hall in Northamptonshire.

President Dole and his PG cabinet in Dole's office at the Executive Building (formerly Iolani Palace). Left to right; Captain J.A. King, Minister of the Interior, President S.B. Dole, W.O. Smith, Attorney General and P.C. Jones Minister of Finance.

Papa kept Kaiulani informed of these events:

June 19, 1893

I have nothing to write that will please you. The PGs have moved into the Palace which I think is a shame, but I hope the day is not far distant when they will have to go out for good—things look better, still we do not know what the US Govt. will do.

I cannot make out what the end will be. I do not think we will be annexed, still there are a great many working against the Monarchy. A Republic would be worse than Annexation. I am in hopes that Mr. Blount will do what is right, and Mr. Cleveland has the reputation of being both an able and upright man.

June 21, 1893

We heard yesterday from a sailing visitor that Thurston has been accepted as Minister from Hawaii by the President. I was rather in hopes the US Govt. would not receive him—still they may not have been able to do otherwise.

June 29, 1893

Spreckels will leave and I hope will go on to Washington. He is strong on our side and will do all in his power for the restoration of the Monarchy.

By August 8, 1893, Commissioner Blount had completed his report on the situation in Hawaii and was returning to Washington.

A huge crowd of Hawaiians came to the wharf to bid farewell to Blount and his wife, who boarded the ship with flower *leis* stacked around their necks.

The PG band also turned out to bid farewell to the departing "President's Man", but their attitude was vastly different from the *aloha* of the Hawaiians.

The Provisional Government had firmly adopted "Marching Through Georgia" as their theme song and, delighted with their choice, they used every opportunity to play it.

Now they lustily struck up their favourite tune, apparently considering it an appropriate (but not very subtle) insult to "Paramount Blount" who was a former officer in the Confederate Army.

On reaching Washington, Blount reported to the U.S. Senate that "A great wrong has been done to the Hawaiians", who were "overwhelmingly opposed to Annexation." He suggested that "their legitimate government should be restored."

President Cleveland subsequently asked Congress to "devise a solution consistent with American honour, integrity and morality."

The PGs began a newspaper called the *Star*, edited by Dr. J.S. Mc-Grew, a physician of Honolulu, who was widely known as the "Father of Annexation".

Papa wrote on August 23:

The newspapers here are simply dreadful. The Annexation Club is printing the most bitter things about us. I am glad you do not see the Star.

On September 12, Kaihulani wrote to her Aunt from the Yews:

My Dear Aunt,

How you must hate the sight of the Central Union Church. What a shame that a house of worship should be turned into a spy tower. I suppose it is wiser for you to remain at Washington Place, but how you must long to get away to some other place. If I was in your place, I am afraid I should pine away and die—I could not stand it—I am so tired of waiting—

By the time this reaches you it will be my birthday. I hope that you will remember me away from my relations and friends.

Soldiers were billeted in both Central Union and Kawaiahao churches.

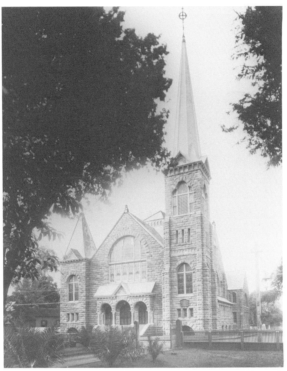

Cental Union Church which was used as a "spy tower" by the PGs. Soldiers were billeted here and in Kawaiahao Church.

Kawaiahao Church.

I am getting to be quite a good needlewoman. Now things have gone wrong, my money matters are in a muddle. I am sure I do not know what I shall do if the PG don't give me some money. We were never very well off - I have to make $500 a year buy everything I need except my food and lodging—I have never been in debt till now.

I will try and be cheerful but I am so homesick! There is no disguising the fact.

Annie Cleghorn wrote to Kaiulani on the same day:

Well Kaiulani dear, from all accounts it seems as though your Aunt will be restored.

She has behaved remarkably well through all the insults that have been heaped upon her. She has been blackguarded right and left. I hope she will remember those who rejoiced and helped in the overthrow. They always professed to be great friends of Royalty.

We have no American Minister here at present. I expect the next one will bring the news.

November of 1893 saw much unrest in Honolulu following attempts to restore Liliuokalani to the Throne. Her life was threatened many times.

To Kaiulani from her Aunt, November 6, 1893:

You may understand how much your father and I had to go through, but there is nothing like being self-possessed and you ought to practice it. Think before you say or act and keep cool at all times. It has been the means of guiding my actions through all these nine months and from all I hear has had a good effect on the people that no blood has been shed, and will end in good results for us. Patience and endurance will always have its reward. I have not much time to write as everything around us seems to be in commotion. The American Minister calls on the PG this morning at eleven—will present his credentials. His name is Willis. He and wife and son arrived last Saturday by the Australia. He is the one who holds our future destiny in his hands.

Meanwhile the Bulletin asked its readers, "What is a PG, since they are neither American nor Hawaiian?"

Central Union Church on South Beretania Street, Honolulu in the 1890's.

The year 1894 in Honolulu was a year of suspense and suspicion with the feeling that trouble was always just ready to erupt.

Everyone was being spied on for the slightest hint of disloyalty to the PGs and every *luau* held by Hawaiians was suspected of being a "Royalist Meeting."

By this time, many foreigners who had formerly supported the PGs regretted the overthrow of the Monarchy and detested the suspicious nature of the government that now reigned in its place.

Finally all large gatherings were forbidden by the Republic of Hawaii.

Waikiki in the 1890's

aiulani was five years old when her uncle King Kalakaua visited Japan on his trip around the world in 1881. It was a trip designed to declare Hawaii a sovereign nation amongst the other nations of the world and it also made him the first King to circumnavigate the globe.

His Majesty was very impressed with the manners and appearance of a 15 year old Prince whom he met at a Japanese Training School where young men were rigorously prepared for military careers.

Komatsu was a nephew of the Mikado, Emperor of Japan, and the political possibilities of an alliance between the Prince and Kaiulani loomed in Kalakaua's mind.

Kaiulani's uncle, King David Kalakaua.

Princess Kaiulani

On impulse, the Hawaiian King sought a private audience with the Japanese Emperor and, after a formal tea ceremony at the Imperial Palace, he proposed the future marriage of the two young people.

In wanting to unite the Thrones of Hawaii and Japan, Kalakaua foresaw that Japan's powerful navy would make an impressive ally in the defense of his tiny Kingdom against usurpation by other nations, and especially America, whose citizens in Hawaii already had too much control of the economics and politics of Hawaii.

On the other hand, the islands were strategically placed in the Pacific for coaling and trading purposes and offered fresh land for homesteading and commercial pursuits.

The conversation continued between the two Rulers with many veiled allusions to all of the benefits of such an alliance.

The Emperor's countenance was stoic as he neither declined nor accepted, but pointed out that Prince Komatsu was already betrothed, hinting, however, that engagements can sometimes be broken.

(After Kalakaua's return to Hawaii, the proposal was politely declined in a letter from Prince Komatsu himself who regretted that he was already betrothed.)

Liliuokalani

Thirteen years later, when Queen Liliuokalani was desperately searching for support in her fight against Annexation, she wrote of the proposal to Kaiulani who apparently had not heard of it before.

In a long letter written from Washington Place, the Queen spoke of both Kaiulani's and Hawaii's future.

My Dear Niece,

Your father called the other day and kindly handed me your note, and I am so glad to hear from you. It is true that many reports have been circulated in the newspapers about my restoration, and in fact many thought it was already settled, but many causes arose that prevented its immediate accomplishment, but I suppose you will have read of it by this time and everything connected with our situation by the President's Message to the Senate and Congress. The delay is unfortunate but the President has said the wrong must be righted, and so it will have to be as according to my protest, everything has been sifted by able men specially appointed to investigate our affairs and their statements have proved satisfactory that the "Queen has done us wrong, but that the American Minister Stevens has done a great wrong." So my dear child we are only waiting for the "good news", then you may come home. It has been a weary waiting and everybody seems disheartened almost with the waiting. Business is dull, no money circulating and those who have it will not spend because of the present government—as everything done now is illegal and it would be a loss to them or parties venturing to spend.

You have asked me a direct question and I must be candid with you in regard to Prince David. I had not thought of mentioning to you about your future until the proper moment arrived but as you already mention it, it is best you should marry one or the other of the Princes, that we may have more aliis. There are no other aliis whom they (the people) look to except Prince David or his brother who would be elegible to the Throne, or worthy of it, and they turn to these two aliis that there may be more aliis to make the Throne permanent according to the Constitution. To you then depends the hope of the nation and unfortunately we cannot always do as we like, in our position as ruler and which you will have to be some day. In some things our course and actions will have to be guided by certain rules and which could not be avoided. I am pleased to see your candor in regard to Prince David —it is good to be candid.

The last part of the Queen's letter discussed the Japanese Prince:

I have to mention another matter, one which I think you ought to know and I hope you will write at your earliest chance and inform me what your opinion is in this matter. When your uncle, the late King was living, he made arrangements that you should be united to one of the Japanese Princes. He is the nephew to the Emperor of Japan. It seems that the young Prince was here in the Naniwa on her first trip last year, but our position was such that he could not present himself, so I have not seen him. I understand now that the Prince is in England being educated so you may meet him on your return. I do not know his name but should you meet him and think you could like him I give you full leave to accept him, should he propose to you and offer his hand and fortune. It would be a good alliance. They speak highly of his qualities.

And now do not hesitate to open your heart to me. I shall be very glad if such an alliance could be consummated between you two and I shall look forward for a letter from you with eagerness, saying it was agreeable to you, and that you will encourage his suit. Do not wish to get fat. If you could only see me you would not wish to be. I have grown almost as stout as Kahuila Wilcox. I am pleased to know that you have a lady with you whose society is pleasing to you. I hope she will come out with you. The above must be between you and I and not mentioned outside until such alliance could be consummated between you two, and of course you can write me, then it does not matter if it goes abroad.

Your affectionate Aunt,
Liliuokalani
Washington Place, Jan. 29, 1894.

Princess Kaiulani

It took Kaiulani five months to reply to her Aunt:

10 Beaumont Street, London W.
June 22, 1894.

Dearest Aunt,

It is a very long time since I received your kind letter. I have often tried to answer it, but have failed. I have thought over what you said in it about my marrying some Prince from Japan.

Unless it is absolutely necessary, I would much rather not do so.

I could have married an enormously rich German Count, but I could not care for him. I feel it would be wrong if I married a man I did not love. I should be perfectly unhappy, and we should not agree and instead of being an example to the married women of today I should become like them, merely a woman of fashion and most likely a flirt. I hope I am not expressing myself too strongly, but I feel I must speak out to you and there must be perfect confidence between you and me dear Aunt.

I have been looking anxiously every day in the papers for news from home, but nothing seems to have happened. I wish things could be properly settled. It is such weary work waiting here not knowing what is happening.

How different the course of Hawaiian history would have been if Kaiulani had accepted the proposal.

Apparently, King Kalakaua and Queen Liliuokalani strongly believed that a marriage between Kaiulani and Komatsu could have been advantageous to both Hawaii and Japan and would have established a Japanese Protectorate over the Hawaiian Islands. As the clouds of Annexation gathered ominously, the Japanese Government would have aided Hawaii in her struggle to remain free, and today the Islands would have been a Japanese ally instead of the 50th State of the United States of America.

Still deeply disturbed by the bad news that kept reaching her from home, Kaiulani wrote to her Aunt of her travels in Germany in mid 1894:

Kaiulani at left photographed with unnamed friend by Tynan Bros. Photographers on the Island of Jersey.

I was quite sorry to leave Germany, everyone had been so very kind to me there, and they have sympathized with us so much. During the last month of my stay in Germany I went to Berlin and there I saw the grand Parade before the Emperor and Empress. It was really a sight worth seeing, there were nearly twenty thousand soldiers and the Emperor had a staff of 100 officers.

Berlin is a most interesting City, it is much more beautiful than London as regards private houses, squares and small parks, and all the chief streets are so wide and most beautifully kept. I visited all the palaces of the Emperors.

Frederick the Great's Palace of Sans Souci I cared least for; it was built after the style of Versailles. He was a very great admirer of the French.

Potsdam where the Emperor stays when he is near Berlin is a most lovely spot about 10 miles from it. It is on the borders of two lakes and all around it is quite wooded. All the best regiments are stationed there and it is altogether a very sweet place.

Always pleased to talk to someone about home, Kaiulani wrote of a visit by Mr. and Mrs. Walker. He was the British Vice Consul to Hawaii, and Mrs. Walker was one of Kaiulani's travelling companions when she sailed from Hawaii in 1889.

Mr. and Mrs. Walker came to see me day before yesterday. I was so pleased to see them. We had such a good talk about Honolulu. She was very much astonished to find how very tall and slight I am, as she always imagined me stout as I was when I was a schoolgirl. I am leaving London on Tuesday to visit Mrs. Sharp and then I go to the Davies family for most of the summer.

At the approach of the holidays she wrote to Aunt Liliuokalani from Southport:

. . . I must just write you a few words to wish you a Merry Xmas and a Happy New Year. This is my sixth Xmas I have spent away from my home, it seems as if I were fated never to come back.

Concerned about her Aunt's recent trouble with her eyesight Kaiulani sympathized:

I know well what it is to suffer from the eyes. Sometimes now if I look very long at anything I get such a headache I don't know what to do.

A description of Kaiulani by a friend in the mid 1890s:

Animated, capricious, headstrong, yes but her vivacity had a certain quiet sadness. Her eyes were too large above cheeks flushed hectically; but such pride of bearing, love of companions and heartfelt loyalty of feeling for her native Hawaiians.

anuary 3, 1895, saw bloodshed in Hawaii. Fighting erupted near Diamond Head between loyal Hawaiian rebels and the Government troops who set up field artillery in Kapiolani Park.

The Hawaiians were beaten and lay wounded and dying on the slopes of Diamond Head.

After this uprising, more than a hundred Hawaiian Royalists were thrown in jail and on January 16, almost two years to the day from the time she was asked to abdicate, Queen Liliuokalani was placed under arrest.

She was taken into custody at Washington Place then driven under guard to Iolani Palace where she was imprisoned.

She later wrote: "My crime was that I knew my people were conspiring to throw off the yoke of the oppressor."

The Queen also wrote that, after being arrested, she glanced back through the window of the carriage that drove her away and saw Chief Justice Judd of the Supreme Court entering Washington Place.

January 16th 1895 saw Queen Liliuokalani entering the rear door of Iolani Palace as a prisoner, in the custody of R.P. Waipa, A.M. Brown and Col. Fisher. The Queen remained imprisoned in the Palace until Sept. 7, 1895.

Queen's Marshal, Charles B. Wilson.

All of the Queen's personal retainers and servants at Washington Place were also thrown into prison. They later told of their outrage as they watched the Chief Justice rummaging through the Queen's private papers, her bureau drawers and her safe until he found her diaries. He then began to read them until, feeling the scornful eyes of the staff on him, he stuffed the books into his pockets and left the house.

A week after her arrest, Charles Wilson brought for the Queen's signature a document of Abdication which had been prepared by the Provisional Government.

She hesitated and then reluctantly signed as she was told, "just plain 'Liliuokalani Dominis'."

Writing later of her experiences during those dark days, the Queen said that she hoped *"By signing this paper all those who had been arrested, all of my people now in trouble by reason of their love and loyalty toward me, would be immediately released. . . the stream of blood ready to flow could by stayed by my pen."*

On September 7, 1895, Liliuokalani received a Conditional Pardon from President Sanford Dole and was released from imprisonment at Iolani Palace. Placed on parole, she was instructed not to leave the grounds of Washington Place without permission from the PG.

In 1896, the Queen received a full pardon from Dole and quietly began to make plans to leave for America to continue the fight for restoration of her Throne. January of 1897 found her settled in Washington D.C. at the Shoreham Hotel.

President Sanford Ballard Dole with members of his provisional government in 1895. Left to right: Messrs. Damon, King, Dole, Thurston, F.M. Hatch and W.O. Smith.

Princess Victoria Kaiulani

n the late 1890's, during one of their visits to the South of France, Kaiulani and her father befriended a young man, Nevinson William de Courcy (nicknamed Toby).

The son of an English Baron, Toby was a qualified architect and civil engineer and was regarded as an eligible bachelor and ideal escort for well-bred young ladies in those Victorian days.

A long correspondence continued between Kaiulani and Toby, who was six years her senior. She referred to him as her "Father Confessor" and in her letters was warm and confiding:

Sunday

My Dear Toby,

Very many thanks for your of the 28th. I also heard from Sib that she had seen you—you both say the other was looking very

Kaiulani's friend and "father confessor" Toby in 1897.

pale and thin. Mon Ami qu est ce qu'il-y-a? Surely you are not ail-
ing! And I trust above all things you are not suffering from mal au
coeur. I have been very seedy. Papa was over in town so he consulted
the Dr. I have been suffering from too much worry!!! So I am to
sleep a great deal etc. Evidently dancing is not harmful otherwise
Papa would have prevented my going to a dance on Wednesday.
Toby I feel so naughty, I have such a nice flirtation on pour le
moment. Don't be shocked, and leave your lecture until we meet
in Menton—it is too good to believe that I shall have the pleasure
of seeing you soon—won't we talk! I have such piles to tell you. I
have Gertie Somers staying with me and also a Miss Brander—we
are about the three biggest flirts you could find, so we simply have
a lovely time. Just fancy Pa went to London on Tuesday last and
returned yesterday. We had quite a nice time by ourselves!!!

"We are about the three biggest flirts you could find. . ."

It is decided we start on the 30th and reach Menton Jan 1
rather a ghastly day to reach a place. I had a letter from Lilian
Kennedy. She seems to be having a perfectly A.1. time—fancy—they
went to a luncheon, she and her Ma—and 7 men were invited to
meet them. There weren't any women in the place. Do you think
you'd like to live there?

I am quite shocked to think that you should long for "Ab-
sinthe". We intend going to the Louvre again—you see Fat George
is the attraction. Madam van Asbeck is there again. Do you know
her? She was chiefly conspicuous by the absence—I should like to
see that charade. I think it must be rather fine! I did not know
you could do that sort of thing!

An excited, scribbled note asked Toby to bring all the men he knew
to the dance that night.

Dear Toby
Come to the dance tonight at 9. & bring Mr Whitlock & any other men you know. Simply

An excited scribbled note asked Toby to bring all the men he knew to the dance...

Menton on the French Riviera where Kaiulani and her father rented the Villa Dimure au Cap for holidays in 1895, 1896 and 1897.

Photo French Government Tourist Office

More to Toby from Ravensdale, the Davies' new house at Tunbridge Wells, written July 4th, 1897:

I have not left for Scotland as you will see by the direction, instead I am wending my way Jerseywards. I start on Monday with Elise, and Papa will join us in a week or ten days. He intends going down to Bournemouth to see the Bishop of Honolulu, and also. . .? The fact of the matter is, he intends taking a little jaunt around the country and enjoy himself.

I shall find it very dull in Jersey as my particular "amusement" is in Woolwich for the summer. Is it not provoking? It is just my luck when I am dull not to have anything on hand.

I have lived on milk for the past two months, and am not taking very much exercise. Consequently I am growing fairly fat. I think I can stand a little more flesh on my bones, still I don't want to grow fat, it is so vulgar you know. Another reason I am growing stout, I have not been able to be up to any of my larks. I've quite got out of the way of flirting! I don't believe I could do it to save my skin. Now, don't laugh!

I am really feeling very much better, but have still to be very careful. I was so annoyed a few days back. I managed to get down for breakfast and stayed up fairly late in the evening, having also played croquet during the afternoon, when on my way to bed, I again had one of my fainting fits. It showed me that I must be more careful, but all the same it is very hard lines, and I hate posing as an invalid.

Where are you going to spend your Summer? There is some talk of my going over to pay my revered Aunt a visit, but as yet things are extremely undecided. They talk of Annexation, but whether they will get it is quite another thing. However, things are in a very bad way out there, and I am now pretty certain that we shall never have back our own again. . . I am really rather sorry the way the whole thing has finished up, much better have a republic than to lose our nationality altogether. . . I am very sorry for my people, as they will hate being taken over by another nation.

If I went over to see my Aunt I would only stay about three weeks there and return again here. My ex-Guardian is going out to Hawaii the latter part of September. He has a great deal of interest in sugar, and he seems anxious about it. He may think it advisable for me to return home the end of this Winter.

The Louvre in Paris.

My Dear Toby

I am really ashamed of myself for having delayed so long in acknowledging your letter. I thank you very much for your kind wishes on my birthday—I laughed very much when I thought of my other birthday—what fun we had that night!

At last we have got back to our little Jersey home. I was quite glad to get back though the trees are all bare, and the weather far from nice—still, it is the one place that I can boss the show, so to speak. I am feeling very dull indeed. Papa has a bad cold, and is consequently in the vilest of tempers. It is most unfortunate as he has been free from colds for so long. He has an idea that he is going to pip which is most annoying—however one must put up with these little annoyances.

Photo Mr. and Mrs. T.A.K. Cleghorn

Oil painting of Mrs. Rooke's house LaChaire at Rozel, Jersey where Kaiulani spent many holidays. She brought this painting home. . . it was signed "From your friend Mrs. Walton, 1897".

We spent a week in town, and then stayed a week with some friends at Southsea. I saw the "Prisoner of Zenda" and "A Night Out" whilst in town—I simply howled with laughter at the latter—it was really too funny—especially when the old Papa comes rushing in with a huge red chest protector on. I really thought I was going to have a fit. If you are up in town and want to laugh—just go there. We were pretty gay at the Langham—had a charming suite of rooms, and simply went the pace while we were up.

We are going down to Menton about the 19th of December—George O'Dell is there already—I am looking forward to seeing you, my Father Confessor—I hope we may have a pleasant Winter. I think Mrs. Suggett will join us—without Jean Erls—your particular friend. I am very fond of Mrs. Suggett—"if you want me—I'm just here!", her particular phrase. . .

One of my young men came out to see me yesterday—I am supposed to be polishing him off—I can't make up my mind to do so just yet must have a little more fun as my fling is limited—I intend to get as much amusement this winter as I possibly can. There is a possibility of my being married in April to a man I don't care much for either way—rather a gloomy outlook—but "noblesse oblige"—I must have been born under an unlucky star—as I seem to have my life planned out for me in such a way that I cannot alter it. Do you blame me if I have my fling now—better now than afterwards.

My engagement is a "great secret"—approved of by Mr Davies and my Father—it is being kept secret for political reasons. Personally I think it wrong like this, as it is unfair to the men I meet now—especially if they take any interest in me.

I am not feeling at all fit, as I had two teeth taken out on my birthday. My jaw was fearfully cut up trying to remove the bits as they splintered. I have had a very bad time of it, as you may fancy. I hope I shall soon get one of your cheery letters, that is if you have nothing else to do.

With love from Papa and myself
Believe me
Yours ever sincerely,
KAIULANI OF HAWAII
Saturday.

Rozel, Jersey. Kaiulani stayed at La Chaire, obscured by trees at upper left.

The friendship between Princess Kaiulani and Toby de Courcy continued through the years of 1895, '96, and '97, when they both holidayed in Menton, in the South of France.

He kept her letters for the rest of his life.

As for Kaiulani's secret engagement, it was popularly thought that she would someday marry Prince David Kawananakoa, who was a nephew of Queen Kapiolani's and a lineal descendant of King Kaumualii of Kauai. It was as though the engagement had been hurriedly arranged in a desperate attempt to strengthen the badly beleaguered Throne.

Whatever the intent and whoever the betrothed, somewhere along the line of troubled events the plan seems to have been abandoned as no engagement was ever publicly announced.

Excerpt from a letter written by Kaiulani to Toby.

37 Avenue Marceau,
Paris
May 9th, 1897.

My Dear Aunt,

Very many thanks for your kind letter.

Annie's sudden death has been a very great shock to both of us—I can hardly realise that the dear girl has gone. (Kaiulani's half-sister, Annie Cleghorn)

I am sorry to say that I am not feeling at all well.

My nerves are all out of order and I suffer continually from headaches.

I daresay you have already heard of the awful catastrophe which took place here at the Bazar de Charite. I have never heard of anything so fearful in my life. Nearly all of the 117 victims were women and young ones too. There is a count next door who has lost his two daughters, girls of 18 and 19.

What strikes one so is it's being in one's own station of life, the smartest society women of Paris.

The death of the Duchesse d'Alemon throws the Austrian, Belgian and Bavarian Courts into mourning, not counting the Arleans and King of Naples families. Just imagine all those people gone in less than half an hour. And the dreadful agony they must have suffered. I have never seen any place so overcast as the gay City of Paris—you see all the people selling, were connected with the highest aristocracy of France.

I hope that you are keeping well and that you are enjoying yourself in Washington. I am going on the 18th to Ravensdale, Tunbridge Wells to stay with the Davies. I hope the change will do me some good.

The City of Paris.

Meanwhile, eager Annexationists in Honolulu were heartened as Grover Cleveland was ousted in the November 1896 elections and Republican William McKinley became President. He wasted no time in submitting the Hawaiian Annexation Treaty to the Senate in June of 1897.

Word of this event reached Kaiulani and her father on the Island of Jersey where they were holidaying at their favorite retreat. Kaiulani was despondent over the news as it now seemed imminent that Hawaii would be annexed to America.

Archie Cleghorn and his daughter discussed the situation far into the night. Kaiulani felt that her "exile" was now senseless and that she was no longer able to endure her absence from home. Whatever Hawaii's fate might be, she wanted to be there to share it with her people.

The next morning they made plans for her return to the islands.

Princess Kaiulani

Busily preparing for the trip home at long last, Kaiulani wrote to Papa from Scotland:

Johnston Lodge,
Anstruther,
Fife.
August, 1897.

My Dearest Papa,

I wrote to Liverpool on Saturday for ten pounds, as I was out of money. I am going to stay four days with the Barbours on Tuesday 24th. . . their address is Baledmund, Pitlochry.

I shall return here on the 28th. The Somers have asked me to stay with them on my way south, and the Wodehouses want us also. So my idea is to leave here on the 7th and stay with the Somers until the 10th. I thought you might go to the Ws on the 10th until the 14th.

The Davies want us on the 17th until the 20th, the two days we might spend in town.

Lady Wiseman wants me from the 24th for a few days. Perhaps you might go from St. Leonards to stay a few days at Bournemouth and also Brighton, while I go and stay with Lady Wiseman.

I want to stay a couple of days in town to pack my boxes. Have you got the address of the Hotel the Watsons spoke to you about.

May wrote and said she thought twenty four pounds too little —considering we are paying her passage out and back again, I think it extremely nasty.

I am going to write her a sharp letter, because if I have to look out for anyone I must be doing so now.

I hope you had a pleasant journey. I expect a letter from you in the morning. We have had fairly fine days since I came but Scotch weather is proverbially bad.

I am feeling very fit and hope I shall be alright. Have you seen anything of Mrs. Stewart? Please give her my love.

Mr. Davies has sent me a plan of the ship, and also the number of my room. I wonder if I shall be alone.

With aloha from all and heaps of love.

From your loving,
VIKE.
Sunday night.

Another letter from Scotland quickly followed:

August 19, 1897

My Dearest Papa,

You never seem happy unless you are imagining your letters have gone astray—of course I have received all your letters. I don't mention every one or all the dates.

I have already written to Mary and told her that we would pay her fare out and back again. My account is she has not half finished doing up my old things. You must not grumble at the account as I am trying to get all my things, so that I won't need to buy any out there. Besides there are heaps of things that have to be bought for the house such as tea cloths and mats and all sorts of small things. Then there are all the presents. You know quite well that all the children will expect something; besides Mrs. Sproull said I ought to take out a large stock of ribbons, gloves, handkerchiefs and those sorts of things. . . you seem to forget that I may not return for some time.

If we were together now we would probably have a violent quarrel over this, but I am sure you will understand when things are put to you mildly.

You seem surprised at my having any enjoyment at all. I had an offer of the box for the "Geisha" and thought I might take the opportunity to see it. The next night we were invited to see the "Midsummer Night's Dream". I am sure that had you had the invitation you would have gone.

I have sent the list of the linen to Mr. Davies, it will be sent overland. Well I hope you will enjoy yourself.

With love from us all.
Your loving child,
KAIULANI.

All the last minute errands and farewells completed, on October 9, 1897, Kaiulani sailed from Southampton to New York on the first leg of her journey home.

It was seven days before her twenty-second birthday.

On her way home in San Francisco, the young Princess was once again inundated by reporters. Impressed by her beauty and her manner, they discredited cruel rumours that were being widely circulated about her by the Provisional Government.

A reporter from the *Examiner* wrote:

A Barbarian Princess? Not a bit of it. Not even a hemi-semi-demi Barbarian. Rather the very flower—an exotic—of civilization. The Princess Kaiulani is charming, fascinating, individual. She has the taste and style of a French woman; the admirable repose and soft voice of an English woman. She was gowned for dinner in a soft, black, high necked frock, with the latest Parisian touches in every fold; a bunch of pink roses in her belt and a slender gold chain around her neck, dangling a lorgnette. She is tall, of willowy slenderness, erect and graceful, with a small, pale face, full red lips, soft expression, dark eyes, a very good nose, and a cloud of crimpy black hair knotted high.

The writer from the *Call* had nothing but praise for her also:

She is beautiful. There is no portrait that does justice to her expressive, small, proud face. She is exquisitely slender and graceful, holds herself like a Princess, like a Hawaiian—and I know of no simile more descriptive of grace and dignity than this last.

Her accent says London; her figure says New York; her heart says Hawaii. But she is more than a beautiful pretender to an abdicated throne; she has been made a woman of the world by the life she has led.

"Her accent says London; her figure says New York... but her heart says Hawaii..." thus a writer from "The Call" described Princess Kaiulani in San Francisco on her way back home in November of 1897.

aiulani left San Francisco for Hawaii aboard the *SS Australia* and on November 9th, 1897, her ship dropped anchor in Honolulu Harbor.

The greatest crowd ever seen in Honolulu assembled on the Oceanic Wharf to welcome Kaiulani home.

She received friends on board ship for half an hour before descending to the wharf where a landau awaited her. In the company of her father, Miss Eva Parker and Prince David, they drove first to the Royal Mausoleum to visit her Mother's resting place and then to Ainahau where her father had built a fine new house.

Stepping onto the precious soil of Ainahau and surrounded by familiar faces full of love and welcome, Kaiulani revelled in being home again. After getting settled, one of the first things she did was seek out Fairy, the faithful white saddle pony of her childhood, who was now 18 years old. There in the corner of a field Fairy still waited for her. Kaiulani hugged and patted him and then gently mounted the old horse. The ride was not as vigorous as it had been 8 years before, but nothing ever felt so good as the cool breezes from Manoa caressing her face while old Fairy snorted into a canter.

The "fine new house" Cleghorn built for his daughter at Ainahau. It was completed for Kaiulani's homecoming in late 1897.

Kaiulani back home at Ainahau. . . 1898

En route to Honolulu, Kaiulani and her father made a special trip to Washington to see her Aunt, the ex-Queen Liliuokalani, who was herself longing to return to the Islands. She sufered terribly from the extreme climate of the Capital City and was greatly disheartened by McKinley's action in reviving the Annexation Bill. She hoped that, by conducting her cause with dignity and persistence, justice would eventually be done and her Throne restored. If that failed, she would still have to fight for the Crown Lands, which were the traditional inheritance of the Monarchy in Hawaii and the source of almost all of her and Kaiulani's income.

It was the first time that she and Kaiulani had met in 8 years and the Queen was very reluctant to let them go. Shortly after leaving, they received the following letter from her:

October 26, 1897
The Ebbett House,
Washington, D.C.

My Dear Niece,

Your short visit to me has been very pleasant, and we have not ceased to talk of you. I wish you could have stayed a month or two longer at least until the question of the Annexation was settled. I think your presence here would have done some good, but as I knew that you and your father were both anxious to get home I naturally kept quiet.

Another reason was I had not the means to detain you which is another and most important point. During your stay I was glad to know that your heart and that of your father lay in the right direction thet is you are interested in the cause of your people.

Aunt Liliuokalani. . . away in Washington D.C.

For the second time Liliuokalani writes that she has heard that Kaiulani is to be offered the Throne of Hawaii.

Here is an opportunity for me to let you know something which I feel you ought to know—and I leave it for your own good judgement to guide you in your decision. It has been made known to me that it is the intention of the members of the Republican Government of Hawaii to ask you to take the Throne of Hawaii in case they failed in their scheme of Annexation. That you should have nothing to say about the managing—that shall be theirs still, but you are to be a figurehead only. If you were to accept their proposition there would be no change whatever in the situation of the country for the good of the people or for all classes of men or for business advancements. You would only be in Mr. Dole's place, despised, and as he is now, in fear of his life.

You will have a few followers who will love you, but it will only be the 2,600 who now are supporting Dole's Government and still have over 80,000 opposing you. It is through their mismanagement that their Government has not been a success. It is for this reason that knowing their instability they want to annex Hawaii to America. Another reason why their Government has not been a success is the people are not with them and they are fully aware of the fact. So as a last trial they wish you to take it. I have shown you in the above, the danger. Now let me explain you another phase. If you decline to accept the position of Queen which will place you more in favour with the people, the Republic of Hawaii will fall through as even now they can barely maintain themselves, then there will be a call from the people for a "plebiscite", then I say "accept it", for it is maintained by the love of the people.

I think Mr. T.H. Davies and George MacFarlane are knowing of this plan and I know approve of it. George said to me when I was in San Francisco that you and I ought to agree on this matter, that I ought to yield to you as the R. of Hawaii, never to consent to have me reign again, that it were better if we agreed on you. I did not give him any answer because I had no right to. The people's wish is paramount with me, and what they say I abide by. Now my dear Child, for you are very dear to me, I hope you will act wisely for your own sake and be cautious in signing any documents they may present to you, reading over thoroughly and understanding it before hand—for they are the greatest liars, and deceitful in all their undertakings and your young heart is too pure to see their wickedness. I mean the PGs. My Dear Niece, may the Almighty help you. Love to your father and I think it well you should show him this letter.

With Lots of Love,
Your affectionate Aunt,
LILIUOKALANI.

Mr Davies wrote a curt letter to the Queen in November, 1897...

I take the liberty of saying that neither Mr. Damon or Mr. Macfarlane or anyone else has ever conferred with me in regard to putting forward claims on behalf of Princess Kaiulani to the Throne of Hawaii. I am also certain that under no circumstances would the Princess Kaiulani have accepted the Throne except with the approval of Your Majesty and at the joint request of Hawaiians and foreigners.

He refers to the rumour as a "melancholy incident" at a time when those "in faithful service to Hawaii should stick together".

Often called "The Princess of the Peacocks" . . . Kaiulani at Ainahau.

After Kaiulani's return to Hawaii, there was much speculation regarding her choice of a husband. During 1898, she was romantically linked with two dashing young *haoles*. One, the broad-shouldered Captain Putnam Bradley Strong, arrived in the Islands on the troopship, *Peru*. He was a daily visitor to Ainahau and he and Kaiulani went horseback riding and swimming in the Waikiki surf until his ship sailed for Manila.

The second romance involved Andrew Adams, a handsome young New Englander who wrote for the *Advertiser*. Archie Cleghorn liked him so much that he invited him to stay at Ainahau, then found him a job as overseer on a plantation. Adams and Kaiulani were greatly attracted to one another, but they quarrelled frequently and eventually became friends and nothing more.

Most of her close friends felt that the Princess was preoccupied with too many worries to be seriously concerned with romance and, although there were many in love with her both here and abroad, she gave her heart to no man.

On February 19, 1898, Kaiulani gave a *luau* at Ainahau to celebrate the 30th birthday of Davad Kawananakoa, her "cousin", who was 6 years her senior. About 100 guests, mostly Hawaiian, attended and the singing was lusty and long, almost drowning out the sounds of the Hawaiian National Band that played valiantly beneath the banyan tree.

Prince David Kawananakoa,
called "Koa" by Kaiulani.

Feeding the peacocks at Ainahau. . . left to right: Prince David Kawananakoa, Eva Parker, Rose Cleghorn (Mrs. James Robertson) and Princess Kaiulani. Photo taken in 1898.

Just after her arrival home, Kaiulani's first letter to her Aunt Liliuokalani read:

Ainahau,
Waikiki,
H.Is.,
November 17, 1897,

My Dear Aunt,

I must just send you a few lines to let you know of our safe arrival. Since we got here, we have been so busy, what with receiving and getting the house in order, I am fairly worn out.

Last Saturday the Hawaiians came out to see me. There were several hundred, and by six o'clock I didn't know what to do with myself, I was so tired. It made me so sad to see so many of the Hawaiians looking so poor—in the old days I am sure there were not so many people almost destitute.

Before I say anything I want to thank you for letting me use your span. They are splendid horses, and will soon be in very good condition. It is awfully kind of you to lend them to me, and I will take good care of them.

I find the place very much changed. I refer to Ainahau. The trees have grown out of all recongition; it is really a very beautiful house and very cool.

A great many of the haoles have called but I am at home for the first time tomorrow. I dread it as I am so very nervous. I have asked Mrs. Carter to help me receive. It is so kind of her to come all this way out—She and her husband came all the way out the day I arrived.

I eat poi and raw fish as though I had never left, and I find I have not forgotten my Hawaiian.

Well, Auntie Dear, I must close. I will write again very soon, but at present I feel the heat so much, I can't settle to anything.

Goodbye, with much love,
I remain
Ever your affectionate niece,
KAIULANI.

She wrote again to her Aunt, who was still in Washington, on January 5th, 1898. . .

Thank God Annexation is not a fact. The people here are not half so happy as when I first came back—I find everything so much changed, and more especially among the rising generation of Hawaiians and half whites. I think it is a great pity as they are trying to ape the foreigners and they do not succeed.

In 1898, other letters from Ainahau to her Aunt in Washington followed:

Papa and I are going up to stay with the Parkers. We leave on the 23rd of June, and I fancy I will stay there until the hot weather passes and I want to go away before the 4th of July festivities come off. I am sure you would be disgusted if you could see the way the town is decorated for the American troops. Honolulu is making a fool of itself, and I only hope we won't all be ridiculed.

(The 4th of July festivities to which Kaiulani bitterly refers, celebrated not only American Independence Day for the Americans living in Hawaii, but also the fourth Anniversary of the founding of the Republic of Hawaii.)

A family friend wrote that "Kaiulani hid the bitterness in her heart from the public, and strove to do what was expected of her." After the Princess' arrival back in Honolulu from England, she became one of the two vice-presidents of the newly formed Red Cross Society and also quickly involved herself in the work of the Hawaiian Relief Society and other social and charitable enterprises.

To her Aunt she wrote:

I should have written sooner, but writing is such a tax to my head here. I wonder why that is. I don't feel the least bit settled. I suppose it is because the old natives are all dead or married.

I am suffering from the heat, but that is to be expected, but I also have hay fever very badly which is extremely disagreeable, though it is harmless.

Her Aunt's previous letter had referred to "possible overtures" of those in power, but Kaiulani replied that she was mistaken:

> *The people of the Government are not particularly nice to me, excepting Mrs. Damon and Mrs. Dole. I think they are very sorry to see me here, especially as I give them no cause to complain.*
>
> *I am sure you will be very sorry to hear of the death of Mrs. Wilson* (she was lady-in-waiting to Liliuokalani when she was Queen, and was her only companion during her imprisonment). *I was very shocked, as I did not even know she was ill. Poor woman, she was always such a good friend of the Aliis. Such a number of our friends have died during the past few years.*

After a lengthy stay in Washington where she wearily continued the struggle to regain her Throne, Liliuokalani returned to Honolulu on August 1st, 1898, on board the *SS Gaelic.*

Her ship docked at midnight and a large crowd of loyal Hawaiians waited on the wharf to welcome her home.

Their Queen finally appeared at the head of the gangplank dressed in black from head to foot. In a quiet show of support the crowd waited in silence for a gesture of recognition from her. Looking down into the sea of faces, many streaked with tears, the Queen called out in a strong voice, "*Aloha,*" and the peals of "*aloha*" rang out in response.

As she walked down the gangplank and crossed the wharf on the arm of Prince David Kawananakoa, men, women and children wept openly and stepped back respectfully to make a path for her.

In the moonlight Princess Kaiulani moved forward quickly through the crowd to her Aunt, the last living member of her mother's family. They held out their arms to one another and embraced. From the wharf, they were driven in a carriage to Liliuokalani's home, Washington Place, where the driveway was ablaze with torches and the night was filled with ancient chants of greeting.

nnexation Day, long dreaded by the Hawaiians, dawned on August 12, 1898. The ceremony was to take place in spite of the protests of both Hawaii's hereditary rulers and most of its populace.

With the Republic of Hawaii now four years old, President McKinley in Washington set the date for transference of sovereignty to the United States.

Sanford Ballard Dole, the President of the Republic, and Harold M. Sewall, U.S. Minister to Hawaii, busied themselves with plans for a ceremony to hoist "Old Glory" atop Iolani Palace.

The scene at Iolani Palace on Annexation Day, August 12th, 1898 as Sanford Ballard Dole (with white beard) offers the sovereignty of the Hawaiian Islands to U.S. Minister Harold M. Sewall.

The largest American flag the Navy could find was raised precisely at noon on the central tower of Iolani Palace. A U.S. Naval Band lustily played "Star Spangled Banner", while two smaller U.S. flags were jerkily hoisted on each of the corner towers of the Palace.

Within six minutes, the Hawaiian Islands had become a part of the United States and Annexation was at last a fact. The joy that was expected at the scene was strangely absent. Many reported seeing the wives of American officials dabbing at their eyes with handkerchiefs. Even the faces of Sanford Dole and some members of his Cabinet had turned pale during the ceremony, which was mercifully brief. Spectators were seen hurrying away to waiting carriages, apparently with no desire to linger at the scene. It was too sad a time, bitter and heartbreaking for too many.

Frequent showers of rain swept over the crowd.

Three American flags fly on Iolani Palace, August 12, 1898.

The Hawaiian flag is taken down. Editor Edmund Norrie of the Independent wrote: "Farewell dear flag, farewell dear emblem of love and hospitality... of a trusting, confiding and childlike people with hearts that know no guile."

"In front of the Executive Building there were Americans, Portuguese, Japanese, Chinese... but no Hawaiians. The ceremonies had the tension of an execution."
Mabel Craft writing at the scene on Annexation Day.

A writer at the flag raising ceremony wrote:

"When the last strains of Hawaii Ponoi *trembled out of hearing, the wind suddenly held itself back and as the Hawaiian flag left the track, it dropped and folded and descended lifelessly to Earth. The day was cloudy and there were light showers."*

One satirical newsman reported:

"Rumour spread telling there would be trap doors (on the speakers stand) and as the Hawaiian banner lowered, President Dole and his Cabinet would sink slowly from sight, amidst a lurid display of coloured lights and smoke."

After the ceremony a reporter resignedly observed:

"We have slept our last sleep as Hawaiians. Tomorrow we arise as residents of an American territory. We must accept the situation and make the most of it, for it is an irrevocable one no matter what some folks say." He then called on the United States asking: *"Uncle Sam shake! It's your turn to stand treat. The call's on you!"*

Another writer recalled:

*"*Hawaii Ponoi *was being played as the Hawaiian flag was lowered for the last time. Before it ended, the native musicians threw down their instruments and ran away, around the corner of the Palace. . . to weep in private."*

Old Glory is hoisted atop the Executive Building (formerly Iolani Palace.)

While Annexation ceremonies were taking place at Iolani Palace on August 12th 1898, loyal Royalists gathered around their Queen at Washington Place. Princess Kaiulani and Prince David Kawananakoa stand to the left of the Queen (seated).

Photo Bishop Museum

Reluctant to relinquish control, the same faction that overthrew the Monarchy continued to govern the islands for almost two years longer.

Later, Lorrin Thurston openly admitted that there had been a plan by members of the "Committee" to overthrow the Monarchy completely from the time Liliuokalani ascended the Throne.

On October first 1898, Princess Kaiulani gave a lavish dinner in honour of the five Annexation Commissioners appointed by President McKinley. Kaiulani sits far down the table beneath the kahilis held by her attendants.

Having lost the Throne irretrievably, Liliuokalani, with vastly diminished hope, left once again in November, 1898, for an indefinite stay in Washington where her fight would now be to regain the Crown Lands. The confiscation of these lands by the new Government was a severe blow to the Queen as most of her income was derived from these hereditary holdings.

Kaiulani was very upset at her Aunt's departure and, as the *SS Coptic* sailed away with the ex-Queen on board, she fell into a depression. Neither she nor the Queen knew they had embraced for the last time.

Colonel MacFarlane, the Queen's confidential advisor and representative, tried to comfort Kaiulani and lift her spirits by pointing out that the American government respected both their positions and would surely provide an income for the Queen and herself and that she would remain a leader of her people in Hawaii.

Kaiulani quietly replied, "Yes, but I shan't be much of a real Princess shall I? They haven't left me much to live for. I don't talk about it . . . I try not to grieve my father who watches over me so devotedly and seeks to make up to me for all the love I have lost. For his sake, I try not to mind. . . to appear bright and happy. . . but I think my heart is broken."

Colonel MacFarlane added that, when on January 30th, 1893, Kaiulani received the cables that broke the news of the Monarchy's overthrow, her heart suffered a shock from which she never fully recovered.

His statement seemed to be borne out by her letters from abroad to friends and relatives in which she often referred to her "good health" or "good spirits." But, in the years following the arrival of those three shattering telegrams, she constantly referred to never-ending ailments such as La Grippe (influenza), headaches, nervousness, hay fever and a lack of energy. To her Aunt she wrote that she suffered continually from headaches and during her last year abroad, she refused countless invitations because of "indisposition."

Colonel Macfarlane, Liliuokalani's advisor.

A pathway at Ainahau.

From Ainahau, she wrote to her Aunt who was once again installed in Washington. The bitterness she felt at the situation in Hawaii since the American take-over was apparent in her letter:

. . . Daily, we as a great race are being subjected to a great deal of misery, and the more I see of the American soldiers about town, the more I am unable to tolerate them, what they stand for and the way we are belittled, it is enough to ruin one's faith in God. . .

Last week some Americans came to the house and knocked rather violently at the door, and when they had stated their cause they wished to know if it would be permissible for the Ex-Princess to have her picture taken with them. Oh, will they never leave us alone? They have now taken away everything from us and it seems there is left but little, and that little our very life itself. We live now in such a semi-retired way, that people wonder if we even exist any more. I too wonder, and to what purpose?

More and more, Kaiulani looked for excuses to get away from Honolulu, finding conditions there unbearable under the new regime.

Eva Parker's forthcoming wedding at the Parker Ranch, on the island of Hawaii provided Kaiulani with another opportunity to leave Honolulu. On the seventh of December, 1898, Kaiulani and a group of friends sailed on the steamer *Kinau* for the Big Island.

The houses at Mana, the Parker Ranch on the Big Island of Hawaii during the late 1890's. The riders are about to leave for a gallop on one of the many mountain trails.

The Parker Ranch, occupying most of the cool, elevated mountain region of Waimea, was known for its grand way of life and was the center of the Big Island's most important social events.

From the tone of her latest letter to her father, Kaiulani enjoyed attending Eva Parker's enormous wedding at Mana (the seat of the Parker Ranch) and the many holiday festivities that followed.

In the first week of the New Year, 1898, guests began to leave the ranch and return to their respective islands. But, Kaiulani was reluctant to return to Honolulu and stayed on at Mana with other wedding guests that tarried.

The Parker Ranch where Princess Kaiulani took her last ride. . .

In the middle of January, a group from the ranch formed a riding party and rode off into the cold air and soft green hills characteristic of Waimea. The group was caught in a sudden downpour and drenched before they were able to don the raincoats attached to their saddles.

The saturating rain of Waimea blows sideways like an icy knife.

Rather than cover up, Kaiulani pulled her coiled hair loose and went galloping into the storm.

Her friends called out to her to be sensible and cover up, but with a fatalism that had lately become a part of her makeup, she replied, "What does it matter? What have I got to live for?"

Good times at Mana, Parker Ranch.

Probably Kaiulani's last letter to her father written from Mana on January 6, 1898:

Dearest Pa,

Many thanks for your letter. I am glad to know you have been enjoying yourself. You seem quite gay with your reception for the officers. I hope it will be successful—I hear the little men are rather nice. Tho' they don't speak much English.

Of course I don't mind lending Ainahau to any of our own friends. I only regret I won't be there to attend the reception. We are all well and it goes without saying we are enjoying ourselves immensely—

We had more than enough fun at the Ball in Waimea. All the people were in their best clothes, and had on their best manners. The Jarretts asked us to it, and they provided supper for our party, and very good it was too. I did not dance very much as I was too amused watching the Country Bumpkins.

The last photo ever taken of Kaiulani (left) in early 1899, seated on the steps of the Parker home at Mana with a family retainer.

Photo Parker Ranch

We left at 12 o'clock as there seemed to be an unlimited supply of liquor going around, and I knew the people would enjoy themselves better if we were not there. We went in the only conveyances there are to be had, between Hamakua and this side of the Island. Hardly any springs and the road was a thing to dream of—once I thought sure we would never right ourselves again.

It had been raining all that day (Friday) and Saturday we could not see twenty yards away—the fog was so thick. We left that evening for Mana in spite of the weather. My goodness the rain cut one's face like hair and it was blowing like cats and dogs. We got home at 7:30, wet to the skin, but thanks to a warm bath and warm drink and our dinner, we were none the worse for it.

The men were obliged to stay at the Hotel, and as luck would have it, the night of the dance, Capt. Lydig's luggage got taken to Puopetu. Sam Parker gave it to the man who drove us to the dance and told him to give to C.L. When we came back at midnight we found it still in the carriage. It seems they had all got soaked through out shooting, and instead of going to the dance, Capt. Lydig had to go to bed! I fancy he and Major Nicholson were very much disappointed at their accommodation, which I think was very ungrateful of them, when the girls were sleeping 8 in a room—they ought to consider—there were besides the family, Cupid and wife, David, Stella Cockett, Leihulu, Kitty and Mrs. Robt. Parker, Dorcas Richardson, Capt. Ross Sproull, Capt. L. Maynn, myself and Hilda and Mary, besides the family. . . there have been over twenty-eight ever since the wedding. . . you know about the size of the houses.

Tuesday we rode over to Waipio, got there about 3:30 p.m. There were quite a number of natives called and during the evening the natives came and serenaded us. As there was a good floor we had some dancing. We all turned in about midnight, but they kept it up till morning. The next morning we took a ride around the valley, unfortunately it began to rain, so I had no time to see my land or rather our land. I am sorry as I would have liked to have seen it.

We had to hurry as Lumaheihei was afraid of the Pali being too slippery. I never rode up such a place in all my life. I was simply hanging on by my teeth. We had a splendid ride home, jumping logs and pig holes—

A good many of the party go home today—I mean the native relations. Our plan is to leave for the volcano, taking the Kinau, then leaving for Kailua on the following Monday. . . We get to Hilo on Wednesday evening staying there until Friday at John Baker's place. Go up to the volcano on Friday or Saturday and leave on Sunday for Punahuu to catch Mauna Loa.

David goes down on the Kinau today to bring up the Dowager. Helen and Stella Cockett and Mr. Parker go up with me to volcano. Being a stockholder, Sam can get cheaper rooms there. Eva and Frank spent Xmas with us here.

I want you to send me my money for this month, what is left and also the $40 for January—I may not need it, but I want to have it any way. Please don't forget. (A belated Merry Xmas follows)

Merry Xmas to you all. My Love to the family. I am so very sorry Helen has been so seedy. What was the matter with her? Tell Elsie to send up my holokus without fail. I want them badly. Send me up some Bromo Quinine pills, also get me headache powders No. 75618 from Hollister—We never ordered sardines in November. One dozen bought for my party by Patty.

Our love to you all, and with much for yourself from,

Your Loving
VIKE,

Koa will tell you all news.

On January 24th, the Honolulu newspapers reported that: "Princess Kaiulani is quite ill at the Parker home at Mana, Hawaii. Governor Cleghorn leaves for Mana on the *Kinau* today."

Papa took the family physician, Dr. Walters, with him, to examine Kaiulani.

Anxious about their Princess' health, Honolulu readers soon learned from the newspapers that "Princess Kaiulani is much improved. She and her father Gov. Cleghorn will return to Honolulu on the next sailing of the *Kinau*."

Kaiulani was carried on a litter from the Parker Ranch to Kawaihae and onto the steamer *Mauna Loa*, as the *Kinau* had sailed without her.

By now, Dr. Walters had diagnosed her illness as "inflammatory rheumatism" with the complication of "ex-opthalmic goiter."

The Princess was in great pain throughout the journey home to Honolulu.

On reaching Ainahau, Kaiulani was put to bed in her darkened room and a concerned Papa took up a vigil beside her four-poster bed. Friends called by daily to see her, not minding the long drive from the city to Waikiki.

By the beginning of March, Kaiulani's condition had not improved.

Doctor Walters, puzzled that Kaiulani had not responded to treatment, called in Doctor Miner to assist him and both doctors employed all their medical skills to arrest the rheumatism that was now dangerously attacking the patient's heart.

She had a bad turn on Saturday morning, March 5th, but throughout the day she seemed to show signs of improvement as the doctors continued to labour over her.

The darkened house at Ainahau.

But just after midnight, the relentless illness began its work of prying her from life once again. Kaiulani tried to sit up. Her swollen throat had choked off her voice and she looked imploringly at Dr. Miner through half-closed eyes filled with pain.

The exhausted doctor patted her hand helplessly, and sent for the family to assemble in the sickroom.

Monday, March 6th, 1899—from midnight to 1:30 a.m., Kaiulani's breathing was very unsteady. Dimly, through glazed eyes, she saw Koa, Helen Parker, Kate Vida, her half-sisters Helen and Rosie, and Papa's stricken face leaning close beside the bed.

The clock had laboriously ticked to 2 a.m. when Kaiulani moved convulsively and cried out one muffled word. Some said she called "Mama!" Others thought it was "Koa!" or "Papa!"

Suddenly the whole room was very still.

Kaiulani had died.

For many miles around, anxious people awaiting news of the Princess knew the precise hour of her death, because at 2:00 a.m. her pet peacocks began screaming wildly. Loud and long, their almost human cries pierced the night.

Drs. Miner and Walters gave the cause of death as cardiac rheumatism and ex-ophthalmic goiter. Their opinion was that she might have recovered from either ailment, but the combined assault was too much for one who was never constitutionally strong.

Kaiulani was 23 years and almost five months old at the time of her death.

All day Wednesday she lay in state at Ainahau.

The newspapers were full of reports:

"The servants, many of whom had known Kaiulani since she was a baby, filed past her body, and gave way to uncontrollable grief. Scattered about her as she lay peacefully sleeping, were dozens of orchids and orange blossoms of purest white."

"Out in the grounds, mournful dirges of the band mingled with the wailing of the older natives as their voices rose now and then in the weird chanting of ancient *meles*."

"All day long the beautiful avenue leading to the residence at Ainahau, was crowded with people who came to pay their last respects. Throughout the spacious grounds, groups of Hawaiians were scattered, giving way to true spontaneous grief, as they clung together throughout the shrubbery, and under the banyan."

The main drive into Ainahau

Among the small but loyal band of foreigners who defended the Monarchy was one Joseph O. Carter.

On the death of the Queen's niece he wrote the following letter:

Honolulu, HI
March 9th, 1899

Her Majesty,
Liliuokalani,
Washington D.C.

Dear Madam,

It is with the most profound sorrow that I convey to your notice of the death of your niece the Princess Kaiulani.

She passed away, after much suffering at two o'clock a.m. of the sixth instant.

In previous letters I told you of her serious illness, but until the first of the current month, I entertained hopes for her recovery. As soon as possible after hearing of her death, my wife Liliu and I went to Ainahau and met with the nearly heart-broken father and other relatives. As your representative, Mr. Cleghorn discussed with me plans for the funeral ceremonies. Mr. Dole offered the Throne Room of the Palace for the lying in state of the remains of the Princess.

Mr. Cleghorn decided at once that such a disposition of the remains was impossible in which decision I supported him, but after much thought the offer of a State funeral by the Executive was accepted. Of course I should have preferred a simpler funeral but one which would have been the expression of more sincerity and sympathy. However, reasons were given why the State ceremony should be permitted. Yesterday the remains lay at Ainahau and thousands of people viewed them, including all classes and conditions of our population.

On Saturday next, the remains will be in the Kawaiahao Church in Casket and the public allowed to view them. The funeral will be on Sunday next at 2 p.m. Program of procession and order of exercises not public yet.

I learn since this letter was commenced that Prince David (Kawananakoa) has loyally and generously assumed the charge of expenses incident to the funeral (on the authority of J. F. Colburn) and if I had known of this in time I should have urged a funeral on different lines, one that Royalists could have directed.

Hawaiians are not altogether pleased to see Mr. Dole's officers so prominent in the conduct of affairs. Strangers in this city comment on the wrong done to Hawaiians and their aliis by the American Government in taking Hawaii nei from the hands of Mr. Dole and his government.

Accept from me and the members of my family sincerest sympathy in your bereavement.

Very truly yours
J. O. Carter.

Princess Kaiulani lying-in-state at Ainahau. . . March, 1899

The funeral observances were transferred to Kawaiahao Church.

"The casket of carved koa wood was borne into the church and placed on the bier in front of the platform. Covering the bier was a purple plush pall, lined with yellow silk, over which was spread the yellow feather pall of Royalty."

Princess Kaiulani lying-in-state in Kawaiahao Church.

"Around the bier were arranged the large *Kahilis*. . . Royal insignia . . . some twenty in number."

"Fragrant maile was wreathed around the pillars of the Church, while from the center of the Arch was suspended an emblematic white dove with outstretched wings."

"At the head and foot of the bier on stands were floral crowns. . . one of white carnations and the other of ilima and maile."

"High up on each side of the organ pipes were hung the Royal Standards of Kaiulani and Likelike."

"At all times both at Ainahau and the church, four Hawaiian *kahili* bearers or wavers stood on each side of the casket, silent and at periodic intervals of about 3 minutes, would slowly bend forward their *kahilis* to meet their opposites, and pausing awhile. . . or with one or two slow lateral motions would raise them again and bring them to shoulder."

"Hawaiian songs and chants were heard throughout the night."

"It rained all day Saturday, but Sunday morning, the day of the funeral, there was a glorious burst of sunshine. . . Scheduled for 2 o'clock, people began gathering at 10 a.m. . . . There was a huge crowd mostly on foot, inside and outside the Church."

Bishop Willis of Episcopal Church conducted the service, while the organist played *In Memoriam* written for Likelike's passing in 1887 and not played since.

The interior of Kawaiahao Church decorated for Kaiulani's funeral.

Photo State Archives

The empty carriage in Kaiulani's funeral procession, representing Aunt Liliuokalani who was away in Washington.

Kaiulani was laid beside her mother, Princess Likelike, in the Royal Mausoleum.

The 23rd psalm was chanted by St. Andrews Priory girls.

Two *Kahili* bearers preceded the procession out of the Church carrying two magnificent *Kahilis* of fresh maile intertwined with ilima leis... They were the gift of Prince David Kawananakoa."

27 *Kahili* bearers surrounded the cataflaque. As the casket was placed on it the old Hawaiians began wailing and chanting *meles*.

A large double rope of black and white attached to the cataflaque, extended through the Church grounds and out into the street... 230 Hawaiians who had coveted the honour drew the body of the Princess with this rope, to her last resting place. . . the Royal Mausoleum in Nuuanu.

The newspapers reported: "Amid tolling of bells, booming of guns, the funeral dirge played by the band; the wailing and chanting of the natives; the long procession started on its way to the Royal Tomb. . . through King St. to Alakea. . . Emma St. to Vineyard. . . Vineyard to Nuuanu. . . Over 20,000 people lined the streets.

Princess Kaiulani's funeral procession.

A few days after her death, a local paper wrote:

The fortune of Kaiulani is not a large one. She has been in receipt of an allowance from the Hawaiian Government, and quite recently the best men in the country to a considerable number, petitioned Congress to continue an allowance to one deprived of wealth and exalted position through no fault of her own.

In the weeks following Kaiulani's death, hundreds of letters poured into Honolulu from all over the United States, some offering sympathy to her grieving family, but a great number addressed to members of President Dole's reigning Government accused them personally, often not in the most polite language, of causing the Princess' untimely death.

One letter addressed to Sanford B. Dole, carefully written in copperplate style and accompanied by another page bearing 25 handwritten signatures, was postmarked Atlanta, Georgia. For three lengthy paragraphs it ramblingly scolded Dole and his "puppets" for "stealing the Princess' Royal inheritance" and "snatching away the Throne she was prepared all her life to occupy". The letter closed by assailing "the cheap adventurers who invaded the Hawaiian Islands just to make money".

The letter was signed:

"Princess K's Friends in the South."

Kaiulani's final resting place. . . the Royal Mausoleum at Nuuanu.

Photo Bishop Museum

After Princess Kaiulani's death in March, 1899, the Advertiser wrote of her:

"Everyone admired her attitude. They could not do otherwise. Her dignity, her pathetic resignation, her silent sorrow appealed to all. The natives loved her for her quiet, steadfast sympathy with their woe, her uncomplaining endurance of her own. The whites admired her for her stately reserve, her queenly display of all necessary courtesy while holding herself aloof from undue intimacy. It was impossible not to love her. . ."

Plaque marks Kaiulani's birthplace now the site of the Pacific Club on Queen Emma Street in downtown Honolulu.

Dress handmade by Kaiulani after she returned from Europe.

Kaiulani's gold watch decorated with blue enamel.

Oil painting by Kaiulani

Oil painting by Kaiulani

Kaiulani's gold buckle inscribed inside "From Koa" (Prince David Kawananakoa).

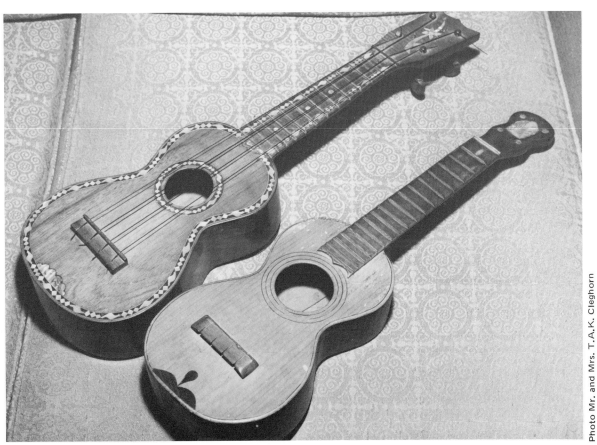

Kaiulani's ukuleles

Lydia Aholo was born in Honolulu in 1878 and had the distinction of being brought up at Washington Place by Queen Liliuokalani whom she affectionately called "Hanai". Lydia died in 1979 aged 101.

Lydia Aholo who was brought up by Queen Liliuokalani at Washington Place, remembered Kaiulani as a "warm, considerate young woman. After she returned from England she was just beautiful. . . her hair seemed to have gone a lighter shade. . . maybe the climate. She gave a luau at Ainahau and I was appointed as one of the kahili bearers. . . to wave the Royal kahili over the Princess' head as she was eating. After a few minutes Kaiulani turned to me and my companion and said: 'You must be tired now. Put those things down and come and sit with me and eat something.' "

Miriam Mabel Kalikohou Robertson Lucas was born on March 13th, 1883 in Honolulu, and passed away in 1975. Rose Cleghorn was her mother and she recalls Governor A.S. Cleghorn, her grandfather as "a kind, loving man who took good care of all his family at Ainahau." Mrs. Lucas was 16 when Kaiulani died.

Mabel Robertson Lucas who knew and loved Kaiulani said: "The Princess was a beautiful girl in every way. I remember her sending clothes to us when she was away in Europe; appealing outfits for me and my brothers. David Kawananakoa and Kaiulani were very close, but it was a brother and sister relationship. She was never thinking of marriage. She was politically astute and would have been a great Queen. The other children would be shooed out of the room when the men talked politics, over at Ainahau. But Kaiulani always stayed and talked with her father and his friends. . ."

T.A.K. Cleghorn was born on March 11, 1899
only five days after Kaiulani's death. He is the son
of A.S. Cleghorn and a Hawaiian mother, making
him Princess Kaiulani's half-brother.

"It is with deepest pleasure and in memory of my half-sister, Princess Victoria Kaiulani that I contribute in a small way to this pictorial story, by allowing photos to be made of mementoes which I've treasured and which have long been part of my life, such as her paintings and personal effects.

"My early life, lived at unforgettable Ainahau, with my father the late Governor A.S. Cleghorn, after Kaiulani's death, was a beautiful time. And to have shared much of what Kaiulani had. . . the way she lived. . . has always been a soul satisfying experience, especially for a young, impressionable boy and it has stayed with me always. Other memories fade, but Ainahau. . . and those lovely, happy days will be with me forever. . ."

. . . Thomas Alexander Kaulaahi Cleghorn.

ACKNOWLEDGMENTS:

FOR HELPING ME TO COMPILE THE MATERIAL FOR THIS BOOK
MY DEEPEST GRATITUDE TO:

Mabel Davis of Honolulu, and her mother the late Mrs. Mabel Lucas.
Mr. Richard Smart and his staff at the Parker Ranch.
Clorinda Lucas of Honolulu.
Mr. and Mrs Nevinson de Courcy of Auckland New Zealand.
Napua Stevens of Honolulu.
The Boston Globe Library.
The staff of the Evening Telegraph Newspaper, Wellingborough, England.
Mr. and Mrs. T.A.K. Cleghorn of Honolulu.
Pat Suzuki of Honolulu (HVB).
Muriel Heen of Honolulu (HVB).
Eloise de Rego of Honolulu (HVB).
Agnes Conrad.
Janet Azama and the staff of the State Archives, Honolulu.
The Hawaii Visitors Bureau.
University of Hawaii Library staff.
State Library staff.
Mr. and Mrs. Frank L. Jeckell of Honolulu.
Lynn Davis of the Bishop Museum Photo Library.
Dr. Roland Force of the Bishop Museum
Cynthia Timberlake of the Bishop Museum Library.
Mr. Hunter McNicoll of Auckland (Air New Zealand).
Mr. John Wisdom of Auckland (Air New Zealand).
Jersey Tourist Board, London, England.
French Tourist Board, London, England.
Hotel Intercontinental, Paris, France.
All the members of the Cleghorn family in Auckland, New Zealand.
Mrs. Percy Cleghorn of California.
Iolani Luahine of Kona, Hawaii.
Lydia Aholo of Honolulu.
Eliza Le Gros of Honolulu.

All the source material for this book was gleaned from contacts with the parties acknowledged above. Original letters and microfilm records of newspaper accounts gave me descriptions of historical events during Kaiulani's lifetime, scrawled inscriptions and dates on the backs of yellowing Victorian photographs gave me the identities of players in the drama; and conversations with the few precious people I met who had personally known Princess Kaiulani gave me the incentive to compile this book in the first place.

Kristin Zambucka
Honolulu, July, 1982.